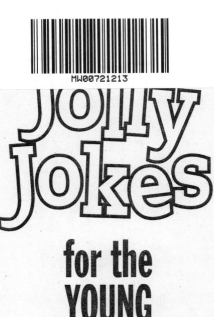

Jolly Jokes

for the
YOUNG
AT HEART

Bob Phillips

HARVEST HOUSE PUBLISHERS

EUGENE, OREGON

Cover by Dugan Design Group, Bloomington, Minnesota

Cover Illustration © Dugan Design Group

JOLLY JOKES FOR THE YOUNG AT HEART
Copyright © 2010 by Bob Phillips
Published by Harvest House Publishers
Eugene, Oregon 97402
www.harvesthousepublishers.com

ISBN 978-0-7369-2617-1

Printed in the United States of America.

10 11 12 13 14 15 16 17 18 / BP-SK / 10 9 8 7 6 5 4 3 2 1

Accountant

Did you hear about the accountant who kept hearing strange invoices?

Acne

There's a new face cream for people over 40. It makes them look younger by giving them acne.

Actions

People may doubt what you say, but they will always believe what you do.

The actions of men are the best interpreters of their thoughts.

Acupuncturist

People who go to acupuncturists are always holier-than-thou.

Adam and Eve

The trouble in the Garden of Eden wasn't caused by an apple, but by a green pair.

Adolescence

Adolescence is that period when many children feel that their parents should be told the facts of life.

Adultery

Adultery is like an adult tree—they both involve grown-up saps.

Adversity

The brook would lose its song if we removed the rocks.

Advice

Advice to all young men: The stork is the bird with the largest bill.

The trouble with good advice is that it usually interferes with your plans.

Socrates was a Greek philosopher who went around giving good advice. They killed him.

Aerobics

They call an aerobics class a re-form school.

Aerobic workouts aren't a new invention. Back on the farm, they call them chores.

Age

Age is mostly a matter of mind. If you don't mind it, it doesn't matter.

You should never trust a woman who tells her real age—a woman who would tell that would tell anything.

An old-timer is one who remembers when a demonstration only meant that someone was trying to sell you a new vacuum cleaner.

The three ages of man: school tablet, aspirin tablet, and stone tablet.

Growing old is only a state of mind...brought on by gray hairs, false teeth, wrinkles, a big belly, short breath, and the all-over feeling of being constantly bushed.

Aleutian

Did you hear about the optometrist who moved his practice to the Aleutian Islands in Alaska? They say he became an optical Aleutian.

Algebra

I can assure you that in real life, there is no such thing as algebra.

Allowances

If you want to teach your kids to count, give them different allowances.

Alzheimer's Disease

Doctor: "Well, I have good news and bad news."

Patient: "Lay it on me, doc. What's the bad news?"

Doctor: "You have Alzheimer's disease."

Patient: "Good heavens! What's the good news?"

Doctor: "You can go home and forget about it."

Amnesia

An amazing fact: When you lend people money, it gives them amnesia.

Did you hear about the psychic amnesiac? He knew in advance what he was going to forget.

An Apple a Day

An apple a day will keep the doctor away—assuming, of course that it hasn't been grown in chemical soil, sprayed with pesticides, and then covered with wax.

Ancestors

Anyone who boasts about his ancestors is admitting that his family is better off dead than alive.

Anesthetists

I heard that anesthetists have a motto. It's "Numb's the word."

Anger

Steel loses much of its value when it loses its temper.

Angry

Q: Which nation in the world is the angriest nation?

A: Ire-land.

An Older Lady Gets Pulled over for Speeding...

Older woman: "Is there a problem, Officer?"

Officer: "Ma'am, you were speeding."

Older woman: "Oh, I see."

Officer: "Can I see your license, please?"

Older woman: "I'd give it to you, but I don't have one."

Officer: "You don't have one?"

Older woman: "I lost it four years ago for drunk driving."

Officer: "I see...can I see your vehicle registration papers please?"

Older woman: "I can't do that."

Officer: "Why not?"

Older woman: "I stole this car."

Officer: "Stole it?"

Older woman: "Yes, and I killed and hacked up the owner."

Officer: "You what?"

Older woman: "His body parts are in plastic bags in the trunk if you want to see."

The officer looks at the woman and slowly backs away to his car and calls for backup. Within minutes, five police cars circle the older woman's car. A senior officer slowly approaches the car, clasping his half-drawn gun.

Officer 2: "Ma'am, could you step out of your vehicle please?"

The woman steps out of her vehicle.

Older woman: "Is there a problem, sir?"

Officer 2: "One of my officers told me that you have stolen this car and murdered the owner."

Older woman: "Murdered the owner?"

Officer 2: "Yes. Could you open the trunk of your car, please?"

The woman opens the trunk, which is empty.

Officer 2: "Is this your car, ma'am?"

Older Woman: "Yes, here are the registration papers."

The officer is quite stunned.

Officer 2: "One of my officers claims that you do not have a driver's license."

The woman digs into her handbag and pulls out a clutch purse and hands it to the officer. The officer examines her license. He looks quite puzzled.

Officer 2: "Thank you, ma'am. One of my officers told me you didn't have a license, that you stole this car, and that you murdered and hacked up the owner."

Older woman: "Bet the liar told you I was speeding, too."

Any Questions?
A man went to a lawyer's office.

Client: "How much would you charge me to answer three questions?"

Lawyer: "Four hundred dollars."

Client: "That's a lot of money, isn't it?"

Lawyer: "I guess so. What's your third question?"

Apathetic
I've been told that owls are becoming apathetic. I don't think they give a hoot.

Apathy
Q: What is the difference between apathy and ignorance?

A: I don't know, and I don't care.

Appendicitis
Doctor: "Miss Anderson, you have acute appendicitis."

Miss Anderson: "I came here to be examined, not admired!"

April Fool's
April 1st is called April Fool's Day...but I think that April 15th has it beat.

Armed Robber

Did you hear about the owner of a flower shop that was held up by an armed robber? He was a petrified florist.

Arms

"Why do you have so many sleeves on your coat?"
"Why? That's my coat of arms."

Aspirin

Most public schools have rules against dispensing any kind of medication, even aspirin. That has led to the utterance of this educational comment: Schools have the right to give you a headache, but not to give aspirins to cure them.

Atheists

Atheists don't have a prayer.

An atheist's club is really a nonprophet organization.

Audit

The IRS has the perfect gift for the man who has everything—it's called an audit.

Babe Ruth

He struck out 1330 times, a record in futility unapproached by any other until Mickey Mantle came along. But that is not why we remember him. We remember Babe Ruth for his 714 home runs.

Babies

I always wondered why babies suck their thumb. Then I tasted baby food.

Baggage

Pioneers had one advantage over airline travelers today. At least when they rode in covered wagons, they knew where their baggage was.

Balance

Many a man loses his balance when his wife goes shopping.

Bald

One good thing about baldness—it's neat.

Bald men can take comfort in the fact that they don't put marble tops on cheap tables. Unfortunately, they are to be found on antiques, though.

Ball

Have you ever noticed that the person who says, "Well, that's the way the ball bounces" is usually the one who dropped the ball?

Balloon

"I just bought a new set of balloon tires."
"Oh, I didn't know you had a balloon."

Baloney

When politicians get to the meat of the matter, it's usually baloney.

Banana

An apple a day may keep the doctor away, but a banana peel will always attract a couple of lawyers.

Waiter: "How would you like a banana milk shake?"
Customer: "That has real appeal."

Banjo Pickers

Q: If you were in trouble and needed to send someone for help, and you had three choices, who would you send— 1) Santa Claus, 2) An out-of-tune banjo picker, or 3) An in-tune banjo picker?

A: You'd send the out-of-tune banjo picker. The other two are myths.

Q: "What's the difference between a fiddle and a banjo?"
A: "A banjo burns longer."

Q: "What is the definition of a true gentleman?"
A: "A man who knows how to play the banjo, but doesn't."

Q: "What's the difference between a trampoline and a banjo?"

A: "You take off your shoes to jump on a trampoline."

Q: "What's the difference between a Harley Davidson motorcycle and a banjo picker?"

A: "You can tune a Harley."

Q: "Why don't banjo players play hide-and-go-seek?"

A: "Nobody will hunt for them."

Bank

I just read a book with nothing in it—my bankbook.

Anyone who can afford to pay the bank interest these days doesn't need the loan.

Bankers

Old bankers don't die. They just lose interest.

I went to the bank the other day. I asked the banker to check my balance. So he pushed me!

Banking

Drive-in banking was invented so cars could see their real owners.

Baptists

A Methodist minister was asked to bury a Baptist. They had been close friends and next-door neighbors. The request was a bit unusual so the Methodist minister asked the bishop.

The bishop said, "By all means—bury all the Baptists you can."

Barter

Ancient fishing villages used to barter with fish instead of using money. They were the first to use credit cods.

Bathroom Scale

What this country needs is a good dishonest bathroom scale.

Between the Lines

The best way to keep people from reading between the lines is to wear a lot of makeup.

Bicycle

Q: "Why can't a bicycle stand up?"
A: "Because it's two-tired."

When the first bicycle repair shop opened, the owner became the industry's spokes-man.

Bill Collector
Wife: "John, the bill collector is here."
Husband: "Okay, give him the stack on my desk."

Birthday
I gave my son a book as a present, but he doesn't know what to do with it—there is no place to put the batteries.

Her birthday cake had 39 candles arranged in the form of a question mark.

Bleed
In olden times, doctors used to bleed people for every minor affliction…and they're still doing it today.

Blind
Donation giver: "It must be dreadful to be lame. But it could be worse. Think of what it would be like if you were blind."
Beggar: "You're right. When I was blind, I was given many counterfeit bills and fake coins."

Blisters
Some people are like blisters. They don't show up until the work is done.

Board
Q: "Who always falls asleep at the meeting of the board of directors?"
A: "The bored members, of course."

Booking Agent

All my doctor does is send me to see other doctors. I don't know if he's really a doctor or a booking agent.

Books

I read a book from cover to cover and found it very interesting—not the pages, just the covers.

This book was so exciting I couldn't finish it until I put it down.

Author: "I wrote a book and it's going like wildfire."
Friend: "Wow! That sounds great."
Author: "Not really. Everyone is burning it."

Brain

Use your brain. It's the little things that count.

Brainstorm

A brainstorm is when you get an idea that's all wet.

Brain Twisters

If you stop your watch, will you save time?

Is a fireplace a place where you get fired?

Is a piggy bank a bank for piggies?

Whatever became of Whistler's father?

What good is happiness? Can it buy money?

What will happen to Scotland Yard when everyone goes metric?

Where can you buy a cap for your knee?

Where can you get a key to the lock of your hair?

Where does the sun go when it goes down?

Where does your lap go when you get up?

Where does weight go when you lose it? Does Weight Watchers know where it goes?

Who tells a bus driver where to get off?

Whose uncle is Uncle Sam?

Why are there so many holes in swiss cheese when it's limburger that needs the ventilation?

Why does it take four weeks' salary to pay for a two-week vacation?

Why don't you call a flying fish a swimming bird?

Why is it that people who say, "It goes without saying" never go without saying?

Brakes

If your brakes don't work, try to run into something cheap.

Breakfast

"I had the strangest dream last night," the patient confided to his analyst. "I dreamed that you were my mother!"

"Your mother?" echoed the analyst, his interest instantly aroused. "I wonder what provoked a dream like that? Tell me the details."

"Well," said the patient, "I dreamed that I woke up at my regular hour in the morning and came to you for my regular breakfast of three hamburgers and an ice cream soda."

"Ridiculous," interrupted the analyst. "What kind of a breakfast is that for a healthy young man?"

Bennett Cerf

Bridle Shower

Is it true that when a horse gets married, they throw a bridle shower?

Bright

Light travels faster than sound. That's why some folks appear bright until they speak.

Brutality

A young boy about to be spanked:

Boy: "Dad, when you were little, did Grandpa spank you for doing something wrong?"

Father: "Yes, son."

Boy: "And did Grandpa's father spank him?"

Father: "Yes he did."

Boy: "And did Great-grandpa's father spank him, too?"

Father: "He surely did."

Boy: "Well, don't you think it's about time to stop this inherited brutality?"

Building and Loan

"Let's play building and loan."
"How do you play that?"
"You get out of the building and leave me alone."

Bum Steer

"Did you hear about the cow that got a divorce?"
"Someone gave her a bum steer."

Burglar Alarm

The perfect gift for the man who has everything is a burglar alarm.

Business

Last year I opened up a general store, but it failed. Seems nobody buys generals these days.

Yes, that's right. I'm giving you a raise because I want your last week here to be a happy one.

Is there anything so embarrassing as watching the boss doing something you told him couldn't be done?

Button

"There's a button in my salad."
"I suppose it fell off while the salad was dressing."

Camping

People who go camping are too intense for me.

Cannibal

Did you hear about the cannibal who went to a psychiatrist because he was fed up with people?

Canterbury Tales

A student in an English class fell asleep as the teacher was reading one of the Canterbury Tales. *Annoyed when he saw the student asleep, the professor let fly with the book, and it bounced off the sleeper's head.*

Student: "What hit me?"

Teacher: "That was a flying Chaucer."

Car

My car can pass anything on the road—provided it's going in the opposite direction.

Car Alarm

Car alarms are wonderful. They give thieves something to whistle along to while they hot-wire your ignition.

Car Sickness

Car sickness is that feeling you get every month when the payment is due.

Carbon Dating

If rocks aren't romantic, why is there carbon dating?

Cargo

"You always used to say I have a body like a beautiful ship."

"Yes, but since then your cargo has shifted."

Carpenter

Did you hear about the carpenter who caught his foot on the roofing and came down with the shingles?

Cash Flow

Why do people complain about cash-flow problems? It's really very simple—you get some cash, and out it flows.

Castle

"May I haunt your castle?"
"Be my ghost."

Catchy

Did you hear about the new mousetrap that lures mice into the trap with soft music? It plays a catchy tune.

Caution

The only exercise some people get is exercising caution.

Celebrity

A famous singer was doing a benefit for a senior citizens' home. He went up to a group of ladies and sat down with them. "Do you know who I am?" the celebrity asked.

"No," said one of the ladies. "But if you go to the front desk, they'll tell you who you are."

Champion

There is no greater champion than the man who conquers a bad habit.

Change

The best way to get a woman to change her mind is to agree with her.

Charm School

I've been told that charm school is where witches go to learn their spells.

Cheep

Did you hear about the man who put a sign over a bird-house in his back yard? It read, "Cheep Hotel."

Chemistry

Teacher: "Can you tell me, Mr. Anderson, one of the outstanding contributions that chemistry has given to the world?"

Student: "Yessir. Blondes."

Children

Ma, if the Lord gives us our daily bread, and Santa brings presents, and the stork brings babies, then what's the use of having Daddy around?

I don't get the best marks in school, Dad. Do you get the best salary at the office?

Man: "Aren't you afraid that your little boy will get squashed in this crowded elevator?"

Mother: "Not a chance. He bites."

Mother speaking to the waiter at a restaurant:

Mother: "Could I please have a doggie bag for this leftover food?"

Son: "Oh, goody, goody—we're going to get a dog!"

Chimney Sweep

I know someone who cleans chimneys for a living. It soots him very well.

Did you hear about the chimney sweep who lost his balance and came down with the flue?

Chinese Food

Some people love Chinese food so much they'll worship the ground you wok on.

Christmas

By the time I found a place to park, Christmas was over.

Church Bloopers

All members are invited to a potluck supper on Wednesday at 6:00 PM.

Prayer and medication will follow.

Remember in prayer the many who are sick of our church and community.

Reverend Gilbath will preach his farewell message, after which the choir will sing, "Break Forth with Joy."

Pastor Rodgers spoke briefly, much to the delight of his audience.

For those of you who have children and don't know it, we have a nursery downstairs.

The eighth graders will be presenting Shakespeare's *Hamlet* in the small chapel on Friday at 7:00 PM. The congregation is invited to attend this tragedy.

Come early and get a back seat!

Church Bulletin

Ushers will swat latecomers at these points in the service.

Circles

"Why does your dog keep turning around in circles?"
"He is a watchdog and he is winding himself up."

Cleaned Out

Here it is the middle of January, and we're still cleaning up from Christmas. Last week we cleaned out our checking account, this week we cleaned out our savings account.

Robert Orben

Clever

A wife laughs at her husband's jokes not because they are clever, but because she is.

Cliché

I always try to avoid clichés like the plague.

Clock

First man: "I just read a book about repairing your own clock."

Second man: "It's about time."

Did you hear that the clock manufacturer passed away? His lawyer is still winding up his estate.

Coffee

Most people are a lot like coffee—they're either perky or drips.

Coffee Break

Doctors say too much caffeine is bad for you, meaning it's time to put the coffee brakes on those coffee breaks.

Collective Nouns

Teacher: "Can someone in this class give me three collective nouns?"

Student: "Flypaper, wastebasket, and vacuum cleaner."

College

A young man hired by a large supermarket chain reported to work at one of the stores. The manager greeted him with a smile, handed him a broom, and said, "Your first job will be to sweep out the store."

"But," the young man said, "I'm a college graduate."

"I'm sorry. I didn't know that," said the manager. "Give me the broom and I'll show you how."

Mark: "My college has turned out some great men."

Lisa: "I didn't know you were a college graduate."

Mark: "I'm one they turned out."

Sending a youngster through college these days is very educational. It teaches his parents how to do without a lot of things.

Colossal

Father: "Say, son, what does this C mean on your report card?"

Son: "Colossal."

Combination

Why don't they have combination doctor/lawyer's offices so you can spend all your money in one easy visit?

Comedian

A comedian is a man who originates old jokes.

A comedian is a man with a fun-track mind.

Coming in Last

I was running the New York marathon and didn't do very well. I was running in last place and was being harassed by the person who was running second to last. He yelled, "How does it feel to be running in last place?"

I replied, "Do you really want to know?" Then I dropped out of the race.

Committee

When all is said and nothing is done, the committee meeting is over.

Complex

My superiority complex turned out to be an inferiority complex. I said, "Great, that makes me the least of my problems."

Compulsive

Did you ever notice the similarity between compulsive behavior and repulsive behavior?

Computers

Computers will never replace humans until they learn how to laugh at the boss's jokes.

It isn't easy being the parent of a six-year-old these days. However, it's a small price to pay to have someone around the house who understands computers.

Condos

It used to be we couldn't see the forest for the trees; now we can't see the forest for the condos.

Conference

A conference is a gathering of important people who singly can do nothing, but together can decide that nothing can be done.

Confession

Steven kissed me in the spring,
  Robert in the fall,
But Carson only looked at me
  And never kissed at all.
Steven's kiss was lost in jest,
  Robert's lost in play.
But the kiss in Carson's eyes
  Haunts me night and day.

Confidence

Confidence is the feeling you have before you really understand the problem.

Congress

When Congress is in session, you had better place your life, liberty, and the pursuit of happiness in a safety deposit box.

Conscience

A guilty conscience is the mother of invention.

Continental Drift

Maybe no man is an island, but he still tends to get continental drift when middle age sets in.

Conversation

Student: "Is there anything I can do to learn the art of conversation?"

Teacher: "Yes, there is one thing. If you will listen, I will tell you."

For several moments there was silence. Finally, the student spoke.

Student: "I am listening."

Teacher: "See, you are learning already."

Conventions

- The Bald Is Beautiful convention is held in Moorehead, South Carolina.

- The mystery writers' convention is held in Erie, Pennsylvania.

- The plastic surgeons' convention is held in Scarsdale, New York.

- The psychiatrists' convention is held in Normal, Illinois.

- The accountants' convention is held in Billings, Montana.

- The canoeists' convention is held in Roanoke, Virginia.

- The locksmiths' convention is held in the Florida Keys.

- The egotists' society convention is held at Lake Superior.

- The Weight Watchers' convention is held in Gainesville, Florida.

- The contortionists' convention is held in South Bend, Indiana.

- The plumbers' convention is held in Flushing, New York.

- The insomniacs' society is held at Wake Forest University.

- The lawyers' convention is held in Sioux City, Iowa.

Conviction

The difference between a prejudice and a conviction is that you can explain a conviction without getting mad.

Cooked Goose

Nothing cooks your goose quicker than a boiling temper.

Cooking

Yes, honey, it's nice and crisp, but tapioca isn't supposed to be nice and crisp.

This submarine sandwich you made me tonight is starting to surface.

I'm not criticizing my wife's cooking, but last night she burned the potato salad.

Clarabelle is going to cooking school at night. Right now she's studying advanced defrosting.

Have you heard about the new recipe for a sponge cake? You borrow all the ingredients.

Cordless

Cordless phones are great…if you can find them.

Cost

A woman traveling alone on an airplane spoke to a another woman who was traveling with two small children.

First woman: I'd give ten years of my life to have a couple of fine, active youngsters like those.

Second woman: That's just about what they cost.

Cost of Living

The easiest way to figure out the cost of living is to take your total income and add twenty percent.

Two can live as cheaply as one. My wife and I can live as cheaply as our daughter in college.

Country Music

Q: "What happens when you play country music backwards?"

A: "Your dog comes back, you get your truck back, your momma gets out of jail…"

Court

I have lost my trust in the court system. The judge just seems to be going through the motions.

Courting

He who would the daughter win, must with the mother first begin.

Cow

Q: What do they call a cow that has just given birth?

A: De-calf-inated.

Crab

They say a crab is a fiddler on the reef.

Crazy Questions

Are schizophrenics ever really alone?

If a schizophrenic commits suicide, is it considered murder?

Why don't we have any rhetorical answers?

Where do baby storks come from?

If what goes around comes around, then where is it?

How do people with amnesia know that they don't remember anything?

What are the heebie-jeebies? I understand that many people have them.

Does everywhere include nowhere also?

What is another word for thesaurus?

Who audits the Internal Revenue Service?

How long is part-time?

Why do they call it life insurance?

Why do people drive on the parkway and park on the driveway?

How far is farther?

Do scary people ever get scared?

If no news is good news, what's bad news?

What did they call the Middle Ages in the Middle Ages?

Cream of Life

Don't expect to enjoy the cream of life if you keep your milk of human kindness all bottled up.

Credit Card

Everything is credit cards nowadays. The other day I tried to pay in cash and the cashier wanted to see my driver's license.

If someone pays you in cash these days, you get suspicious—you wonder whether his credit is any good.

Crime

The crime in New York is getting worse. I was there the other week. The Statue of Liberty had both hands up.

Critic

A critic is a fellow who goes along for deride.

I have yet to find a man, however exalted in his position, who did not do better work or put forth greater effort under a spirit of approval than under the spirit of criticism.

Charles Schwab

Criticism

For every action there is an equal and opposite criticism.

Cross-country

Did you hear about the cross-country ski race to be held in Sweden? The winner will be the first skier who crosses the Finnish line.

Crossing the Road

Q: Why did the chicken cross the road?

A: To show the possum it can be done.

Cuckoo

Q: What do they call a timepiece in a psychiatrist's office?

A: A cuckoo clock.

Curiosity

A bright eye indicates curiosity; a black eye, too much.

Cynic

An optimist is a father who lets his son take the new car on a date. A pessimist is one who won't. A cynic is one who did.

Daffy Definitions

Accountant	A desk jockey.
Actor	The only ham that can't be cured.
Ad libber	A person who stays up all night to memorize spontaneous jokes.
Adolescence	The age when a child tries to bring up his parents.
Adolescent	A youngster who acts like a baby when you don't treat him like an adult.
Adult	A person who has stopped growing at both ends and has started growing in the middle.
American	A person who knows but never remembers the words to "The Star-Spangled Banner."

A person who knows when and where the pilgrims landed, but has no idea why.

Archaeologist	Someone whose career lies in ruins.
Astronaut	A whirled traveler.
Astronomer	A night watchman.
Autograph collector	A big-name hunter.
Average person	Any person who thinks he is above average.
Baby	An alimentary canal with a loud voice on one end and no responsibility on the other.

Mama's little yelper.

Baby quadruplets	Four crying out loud.
Babysitter	A person you pay to watch television while the children cry themselves to sleep.
Bachelor	A person who can take a nap on top of the bedspread.
Bachelor girl	A girl who is still looking for a bachelor.
Backseat driver	One who never runs out of gas.
Baker	A person who rolls in dough.
Barber	A brilliant conversationalist who occasionally shaves and cuts hair.
Beatnik	Santa Claus the day after Christmas.

Belly laugh	Mirthquake.
Bore	A person who can talk long enough to put you to sleep, but loud enough to keep you awake.

☕ ☕ ☕

	A person who gets offended when others talk while he's interrupting.
Boss	A person who comes in early to see who comes in late.
Boy	A person who gets his hands dirty washing his face.
Bridegroom	A man who spends a lot of money on a new suit that no one notices.
Broker	What you become when you play the stock market.
Calories	Weight lifters.
Capitalist	A person who continues to spend less than his income.
Careful driver	A motorist who just saw a driver ahead of him getting a ticket.
Cashier	A quick-change artist.
Character	What one is called if one doesn't have any.
Child	A thing that stands halfway between an adult and the television screen.
Chiropractor	A doctor who kneads patients.

Commuter	A person who pays short visits to his home and office.
Consultant	A person who is called in at the last minute to share the blame.
Cook	A pan-handler.
Counter spy	A department store detective.
Credit card	The sweet buy and buy.
Creditor	A person who has a better memory than a debtor.
Defender	Part of a car.
Dentist	A person who always bores you to tears.
Desk	A wastebasket with drawers.
Diamond jubilee	When the last installment is paid on the engagement ring.
Diplomat	A person who can put his best foot forward when he doesn't have a leg to stand on.
Doctor	A person you stick your tongue out to.
Economist	A person who knows tomorrow why things he said yesterday didn't happen today.
Editor	A literary barber.
Efficiency expert	A person who spends six years in college learning how to look busy while watching you work.

Egoist	A person who's always me-deep in conversation.
Electrician	A switch doctor.
English horn teacher	Tudor tooter tutor.
Eskimos	Make pies.
Executive	A person who can take two hours for lunch without hindering production at work.
Expert	A person who can take something you already knew and make it sound confusing.
Family man	A man who replaces the money in his wallet with snapshots of the wife and kids.
Farmer	A person who can make plenty of money if he sells his farm to a golf club.
Father	A man who buys the frills, pays the bills, and signs the wills.
Flattery	The applause that refreshes.
Flu season	Hoarse and buggy days.
Forger	A person who is always ready to write a wrong.
Friend	A person who goes around saying nice things about you behind your back.
Gambler	A person who picks his own pocket.

Genius	A person who can refold a new shirt and not have any pins left over.
Gentleman	A person who steadies the stepladder for his wife while she paints the kitchen ceiling.
Girl	A person who will scream at a mouse but smile at a wolf.
Girl watcher	Peer group.
Golfer	A person who yells "FORE," takes six, and puts down five.
Grandmother	An old lady who comes to your house, spoils the children, and then goes home.
Housewife	A woman who, when it comes to housework, likes to do nothing better.
Husband	A person whose chief function is to pay bills.
Hypochondriac	A person who can't leave being well enough alone.
Hypocrite	A person who says he likes doing the dishes.
In conclusion	The phrase that wakes up the audience.
Infant	A household object that gets you down in the daytime and up at night.
Inflation	A drop in the buck.
Interior decorator	A person who does things to your

	house he wouldn't dream of doing to his own.
Judge	A referee between two lawyers.
Juvenile delinquent	A minor who is a major problem.

☕ ☕ ☕

	A child hood.
Lawyer	A person who helps you get what is coming to him.
Lazy butcher	A meat loafer.
Laziness	The mother of intention.
Mother-in-law	Another figure of speech, relatively speaking.
Motorist	A driver who, after seeing a wreck, drives carefully for a few blocks.
Mummies	Egyptians pressed for time.
Musician	A band aid.
Neighbor	A person who advises you about what to buy so he can borrow it later.
Old-timer	A person who remembers when a caller rang the doorbell instead of blowing the horn.

☕ ☕ ☕

A person who remembers when a coffee break was your lunch hour.

☕ ☕ ☕

A person who remembers when a summer vacation was one day at the county fair.

A person who remembers when air pollution was corned beef and cabbage.

A person who remembers when babysitters were called mothers.

A person who remembers when campers were people, not trucks.

A person who remembers when health foods were whatever your mother said you'd better eat or else.

A person who remembers when it took a whole week to spend a week's pay.

A person who remembers when

people aimed to get to heaven instead of the moon.

A person who remembers when people stopped spending when they ran out of money.

A person who remembers when the only garbage problem was getting your husband to put it out.

A person who remembers when the wonder drugs of the day were castor oil and camphor.

A person who remembers when the younger generation used to go to bed before the adults.

A person who remembers when we sat down at the table and counted our blessings instead of calories.

A person who remembers when we used to kill time by working.

A person who remembers when your coffee break came with the meal.

Optimist

A person who keeps the motor running while waiting for his wife to get dressed.

A person who sets aside two hours to do his income tax return.

A person who thinks a woman will hang up the phone just because she said good-bye.

Paratrooper

A person who has to pull strings to stay in his job.

Parking lot attendant

A professional fender bender.

Pawnbroker

The person you have to see after you've done business with your stock-broker.

Pedestrian

A person who is looking for the place he parked his car.

A person who thought his car battery would last another day.

Pessimist   A man who always finds something to worry about once he puts his mind to it.

A man who complains about the noise when opportunity knocks.

A man who is never happy unless he is miserable.

A man who is seasick during the entire voyage of life.

A man who, when he has a choice between two evils, chooses both.

Philosopher   A person who always knows what to do until it happens to him.

Pickpocket   A person who is a wallet collector.

Plumber   A person who gets paid for sleeping under other people's sinks.

Plumber's assistant   Drainee trainee.

Politician   A person who has his hands in your pocket, his mouth in your ear, and his faith in your patience.

Politics	The most promising of all careers.
Psychiatrist	A person who doesn't have to worry as long as others do.
Relative	An inherited critic.
Restaurant chains	Cook-alikes.
Sarcasm	Barbed ire.

☕ ☕ ☕

	Quiplash.
Scientist	A person who is always trying to prolong life so we can have time to pay for all the gadgets he invents.
Sneezing	Much "achoo" about nothing.
Specialist	A doctor who has patients trained to become ill only during office hours.
Taxi driver	A person who drives away customers.
Teenagers	People who express a burning drive to be different by dressing exactly alike.
Twins	Infant replay.
Veterinarian	A doctor who makes horse calls.
Wife	A woman who is a dish jockey.

☕ ☕ ☕

	A woman who reaches for a chair when answering the telephone.
Window shopper	A store gazer.
Woman	A person who is the female of the speeches.

Woman's purse	A velvet-lined junkyard.
Woman's tears	The most efficient water power in the world.
Women's dress shop	A wear-house.
Women's intuition	A suspicion that turns out to be true.

Daydream

Don't daydream on the company's time—you might miss the coffee break.

Dead

People who believe that the dead never come back to life should be here at quitting time.

Decisiveness

Lack of decisiveness is probably a bad trait...on the other hand, maybe not.

Dentist

Did you hear about the guru who became a dentist? He no longer used Novocain to reduce pain. Instead, he started using transcend dental medication.

I was going to go to my dentist for some work, but I lost my nerve.

Dentists take great pains in their work.

Department of the Interior

Where else but in Washington, D.C. would they call the department in charge of everything outdoors the Department of the Interior?

Determination

Bite off more than you can chew,
    then chew it.
Plan more than you can do,
    then do it.
Point your arrow at a star,
    take your aim, there you are.
Arrange more time than you can spare,
    then spare it.
Take on more than you can bear,
    then bear it.
Plan your castle in the air,
    then build a ship to take you there.

Diamond

Some women are so hard, only a diamond makes an impression on them.

Did You Know?

A firefly is not a fly, nor is a glowworm really a worm. Both are beetles.

A Douglas fir is actually a pine tree.

When clothes are dry cleaned, a liquid is used.

☕ ☕ ☕

Camel's hair brushes are made of squirrel fur.

☕ ☕ ☕

Men walk from the knee, and women from the hip.

☕ ☕ ☕

Men strike matches toward themselves, and women away from themselves.

☕ ☕ ☕

Men look at their fingernails by cupping their palms and bending their fingers toward themselves. Women look at their nails by extending their fingers outward.

☕ ☕ ☕

Men nag their wives for what they do, and wives nag their husband for what they don't do.

Diet

There's no use going on a diet if you have to starve to death to live longer.

☕ ☕ ☕

The toughest part of dieting isn't watching what you eat; it's watching what your friends eat.

☕ ☕ ☕

People who say they are going on a diet are just wishful shrinkers.

If you don't worry about your diet, everything may go to pot.

A diet is a short period of starvation followed by a rapid gain of five pounds.

For some people, their diets are all behind them now.

Some people like to follow low-fat diets, and others are members of the frequent-fryer program.

Difference
The difference between a discussion and an argument is whether you're winning it or not.

Different
If you want to be different these days, just act normal.

Discontent
There's a story making the rounds about a man who entered a very strict monastery. Members were permitted to speak only once every five years, and only two words at that. At the end of the first five years, one man appeared before his superior and was granted permission to speak.

"Bed hard," said the man.

He was then dismissed.

Five years later he appeared, and was again permitted to speak. This time he said, "Food bad." He was again dismissed.

Still another five years went by, and he appeared before the same superior. This time he said, "I quit."

The superior looked at him for a long time, and then finally responded: "I expected this. You have done nothing but complain ever since you've been here."

Dishes

An amazing fact: No woman has ever shot her husband while he was doing the dishes.

The best way for a housewife to have a few minutes to herself at the close of the day is to start washing the dishes.

Doctor

My doctor can't be a very good doctor. All his patients are sick.

My doctor has magic hands. Every time he touches me, one hundred dollars disappears.

My doctor is really nice. When he treated me for double pneumonia, he sent me a bill for only one pneumonia.

My doctor is not concerned with Medicare. He never had a patient who lived to reach 65.

My doctor told me I'm in good shape for a man of 60. Too bad I'm only 49.

My doctor turned kidnapper but failed because nobody could read his ransom notes.

Dolphins
Q: What do you call ten angry dolphins?
A: Cross-porpoises.

Down in the Mouth
Patient: "Doctor, I think I swallowed a pillow."
Doctor: "How do you feel?"
Patient: "A little down in the mouth."

Down Payment
Did you hear about the department store that bought a large order of goose-feather jackets? They had to make a large down payment on the order.

Dream House
Why do you call your new home your dream house? Because it cost you twice as much as you dreamed of.

Drive-through

Have you noticed that there's a drive-through for everything in California? They even have a burial service called Jump in the Box.

Driving

Nothing will improve your driving like the discovery that your license has expired.

A young boy was telling his mother about a ride in the car with his father. "Guess what, Mom! We passed two idiots, three morons, four crazy fools, and a whole bunch of knotheads."

Dropouts

The trouble with school dropouts is not that they can't see the handwriting on the wall, but that they can't read it.

Drudgery

Drudgery is working like a dog for money. A hobby, on the other hand, is doing the same thing for nothing.

Drugs

With all the drugs and alcohol people consume today, this could be termed the Stoned Age.

Drugstore

Expensive medicines are always good—if not for the patient, at least for the druggist.

Aspirin is a miracle drug. A year's supply usually disappears in a month.

Dumb

"I'm not as dumb as I look."
"You couldn't be."

Duty

The definition of *duty* is that which you hate to do, but love to brag about.

Earthquake

Did you hear about the wealthy philanthropist who left all his money to earthquake research? He was generous to a fault.

Economics

A study of economics usually reveals that the best time to buy anything is last year.

Economist

If all the economists in the world were placed end to end, they wouldn't reach a conclusion

He's a great economist. He predicted nine out of the last four recessions.

Edge

Lots of people live life on the edge—the edge of the couch.

Egotist

At least an egotist doesn't go around talking about other people.

Egyptian

Q: What do they call an Egyptian bone doctor?

A: A Cairo practor.

Electoral College

You can't fool all the people all of the time. That's why we have the electoral college.

Electrical Appliances

I've been told that the best place to buy electrical appliances is at an outlet store.

Electric Bill

An electric bill has been called the charge of the light brigade.

Embassy

We're having so much trouble overseas that the government has developed a prefabricated embassy building. It comes with the windows already broken out.

Energy Crisis

Because of the energy crisis, fish markets are trying to become more efficient by forming carp pools.

Enormous

Q: What do you get when you cross an elephant with a mouse?

A: Enormous holes in the baseboard.

Eskimo

Two eskimos sitting in a kayak were chilly. When they lit a fire in the craft, it sank—proving once and for all that you can't have your kayak and heat it, too.

Executive

As everyone knows, an executive has practically nothing to do except to decide what has to be done...tell someone to do it...listen to the reasons it should not or cannot be done that way...listen to why it should be done by someone else or done a different way...follow up to see if the thing has been done...discover that it has not been done...inquire why...listen to excuses from the person who should have done it...follow up again to see if the thing has been done...only to discover that it has been done...incorrectly.

Exercise

Too many people get their exercise by jumping to conclusions, running up bills, stretching the truth, bending over backward, lying down on the job, sidestepping responsibility, and pushing their luck.

Exhaust

What most people need is more horsepower and less exhaust.

Experience

Experience is that which allows us to be stupid in totally original ways.

One reason experience is such a good teacher is it doesn't allow any dropouts.

A man who carries a cat by the tail learns something he can learn in no other way.

Mark Twain

Education is reading the fine print. Experience is not reading it.

Some people speak from experience, and others, from experience, don't speak.

Experience is a wonderful thing. It enables you to recognize a mistake when you make it again.

Extreme

Did you hear about the thirsty man in the desert? He walked miles in every direction looking for water. All he found were streams that had dried up. He exclaimed, "I'm tired from going from one ex-stream to another."

Eye

"Have you got something in your eye?"

"No, I'm just trying to look through my finger."

Face-saving

Q: What is another name for plastic surgery?

A: Face-saving.

Failure

Failure is a better teacher than success, but she seldom finds an apple on her desk.

If at first you don't succeed, destroy all evidence that you tried.

Fair Trade

Joe: "I just got a new car for my wife."

Moe: "Now that's what I call a fair trade."

Famous

Anybody who wakes up and finds himself famous hasn't been asleep.

Farmer

There was a farmer who owned a big hayfield. The farmer's son decided to move to the city and earn his living there. But when he got to the city, the best he could do was to get a job as a bootblack at the railroad station. Now the farmer makes hay while the son shines.

Fast

Horse trainers have learned that the best way to make a slow horse fast is to take away his oats.

Father

A father is a person who spends several thousand dollars on his daughter's wedding, then reads in the paper that he gave the bride away.

Favorite Songs of Bible Characters

Noah	"Raindrops Keep Falling on My Head"
Adam and Eve	"Strangers in Paradise"
Lazarus	"The Second Time Around"
Job	"I've Got a Right to Sing the Blues"
Moses	"The Wanderer"
Samson	"Hair"
Daniel	"The Lion Sleeps Tonight"
Joshua	"Good Vibrations"
Elijah	"Up, Up and Away"
Methuselah	"Stayin' Alive"

Federal Aid

Federal aid is like giving yourself a transfusion by drawing blood from your right arm, returning it to your left, and spilling 80 percent of it on the way across.

Feeling Bad

A fellow went to see a doctor, and while he was being examined, he said, "Boy, I sure hope I'm sick."

The doctor said, "That's a bad attitude you've got."

The fellow said, "Well, I'd sure hate to feel this bad and then find out I'm well."

File

"Do you file your nails?"

"No, I cut them off and throw them away."

Finance

Finance is the art of passing money from hand to hand until it disappears.

First Meal

Bride to new husband: "There you are, darling—my first meal cooked just the way you better like it."

Fish and Chips

Did you hear about the two brothers who joined a monastery and then opened a fish-and-chips restaurant? The first brother became the fish friar, and the other became the chip monk.

Fishy

Q: What do you get when you cross a flat fish with George Washington?

A: The flounder of our country.

Every morning, rain or shine, the fisherman would go to sea, and each night, he would tell his family of the tremendous fish he had seen and almost caught.

This fisherman had two sons of whom he was very proud. One was named Toward, and the other was named Away.

One morning he took his sons fishing with him for

the first time. That night, when he returned, he was more excited than ever. "Listen," he told his wife. "you should have seen the tremendous fish we saw today. It was five feet long, and it crawled right up on the beach. But before I could do anything, it grabbed Toward and swallowed him in one gulp."

"Oh, that's terrible!" his wife exclaimed. "Poor Toward!"

"But that's only part of it," the fisherman said. "You should have seen the one that got Away."

Fixed Income

Fixed income is what is left over after you've fixed the washing machine, the television, the car, and the kid's bike.

Flaky

Did you know that people who like to stand outside when it is snowing are considered flaky?

Flirting

Flirting is wishful winking.

Flushing

How do you feel about Flushing, New York?
I think it's a great idea.

Food

I call our toaster "Indian" because it always sends up smoke signals.

Food Prices

If food prices keep rising, politicians won't be the only ones sitting down to hundred-dollars-a-plate dinners.

Fool

They say there's no fool like an old fool, but you've got to remember that they've been practicing their whole lives.

Never argue with a fool. Onlookers may not know which is which.

Forever

If you want to write something that will live forever, sign a mortgage.

Forget

Why is it that people who drink to forget never forget to drink?

Fountain of Youth

Maybe there is no fountain of youth, but a couple of drinks will make most people less mature.

Fractions

Did you know that five out of three people have trouble with fractions?

Free Speech

The main reason politicians champion free speech in this country is that they're not going to listen to what we say anyway.

Freudian Slip

A Freudian slip is what you buy at a psychoanalytical lingerie shop

Friend

If you lend a friend five dollars and never see him again, it was worth it.

He who seeks friends without faults stays forever without friends.

Friends are people who stick together until debt do them part.

A friend is a person who goes around saying nice things about you behind your back.

Prosperity begets friends; adversity proves them.

A friend is one before whom I may think aloud.

Ralph Waldo Emerson

Fundraiser

Two men were chatting about their children, who were away at school.

"What does your son plan to do when he finishes college?" the first asked.

"He hasn't decided yet," said the other. "But judging from his letters, he would make an excellent professional fund-raiser."

Garden

Last year, we ate our whole garden in one meal.

There is only one thing that will make your lawn look as nice as your neighbors'—snow!

Gardener

Give a gardener an inch, and he'll take a yard.

Garden Slug

I don't want to say televised Senate sessions are boring, but most folks would prefer to watch a PBS special about garden slugs.

Gates of Heaven

A woman arrived at the gates of heaven. While she was waiting for Saint Peter to greet her, she peeked through the gates. She saw a beautiful banquet table. Sitting all around were her parents and all the other people she had loved and who had died before her. They saw her and began calling greetings to her: "Hello! How are you? We've been waiting for you!"

When Saint Peter came by, the woman said to him, "This is such a wonderful place! How do I get in?"

"You have to spell a word," said Saint Peter.

"Which word?" the woman asked.

"Love."

The woman correctly spelled *love*, and Saint Peter welcomed her into heaven.

About a year later, Saint Peter came to the woman and asked her to watch the gates of heaven for him that day. While the woman was guarding the gates, her husband arrived.

"I'm surprised to see you," the woman said. "How have you been?"

"Oh, I've been doing pretty well since you died," her husband told her. "I married the beautiful young nurse who took care of you while you were ill. And then I won the multistate lottery. I sold the little house you and I lived in and bought a huge mansion. And my wife and I traveled all around the world. Today we were on vacation in Cancun, and I went water skiing. I fell and hit my head on a rock, and here I am. What a bummer! How do I get in?"

"You have to spell a word," the woman said.

"Which word?" her husband asked.

"Czechoslovakia."

Generation Crisis

A generation crisis in reverse occurred when a teenager drove his car into the garage and ran over his father's bicycle.

Geologist

A geologist is a fault finder.

Getting Old

You know you're getting old when you don't go out at night because your back already went out.

You know you're getting old when your entire future is behind you.

You know you're getting old when it takes longer to rest than it does to get tired.

You know you're getting old when you still have a lot of gas in the old tank but you need a new ignition system.

You know you're getting old when you finally know all the answers but you can't remember the questions.

You know you're getting old when they start playing your favorite songs on the piped-in music at the supermarket.

You know you're getting old when you go to your high school reunion and it looks like you're at an archaeological dig.

You know you're getting old when bingo is a way of life instead of a dog's name.

You know you're getting old when, instead of avoiding temptation, it avoids you.

You know you're getting old when your rock 'n' roll turns to walk 'n' stroll.

Giving

What you keep to yourself, you lose; what you give away, you keep forever.

Global Warming

Scientists have just discovered that the greenhouse effect has radically worsened due to all the politicians' blowing nothing but hot air about the environment.

Gnawing

By gnawing through a dike, even a rat may drown a nation.

Edmund Burke

Golf

It's not that I really cheat at golf. I play for my health, and a low score makes me feel better.

If you watch a game, it's fun. If you play it, it's recreation. If you work at it, it's golf.

Golf Handicap

I've been told that a golf handicap is when you are playing golf with your boss.

Good Mileage

You can't beat Christopher Columbus at getting good mileage. Look at all the miles he got out of three galleons.

Good News

This is the only country in the world where the government argues over the size of the color TV set that a family on welfare should get.

This is the only country in the world where people who go to pick up their unemployment check have a parking problem.

Good Old Days

The good old days were when a juvenile delinquent was a boy who played the saxophone too loud next door.

Good Sport

The worst thing about being a good sport is you have to lose to prove it.

Gossip

Q: What is the definition of *gossip*?

A: Mouth-to-mouth recitation.

Gossip is called, "Letting the chat out of the bag."

An effective gossip is a person who knows how to keep a secret…in circulation.

I will never repeat gossip, so please listen carefully the first time.

Government

Employee: "May I destroy these old government files?"

Employer: "Yes, provided you make a photocopy of each file before you destroy it."

Government Job

"I heard you applied for a government job. What are you doing now?"

"Nothing. I got the job."

Graduate

The graduate with a science degree asks, "Why does it work?"

The graduate with an engineering degree asks, "How does it work?"

The graduate with an accounting degree asks, "How much does it cost?"

The graduate with a liberal arts degree asks, "Do you want fries with your hamburger?"

Grammar

Teacher: "What is the opposite of sorrow?"

Student: "Joy."

Teacher: "What is the opposite of misery?"

Student: "Happiness."

Teacher: "Good, now give me the opposite of woe."

The student thought for a moment, then said, "Giddy-up."

Greens Fee

Did you hear about the baby who was born on the lawn in front of the hospital? The doctor, however, still charged $300 for use of the delivery room. Understandably, the new parents objected. Because of this, the doctor changed the bill to read: "Greens fees, $300."

Groom

Naturally, no one gives the groom a shower—he's all washed up anyway.

Grouch

A grouch spreads cheer wherever he doesn't go.

Growl

If you growl all day, it's only natural you'll feel dog tired at night.

Habits

If there's anything harder than breaking a bad habit, it's trying to refrain from telling people how you did it.

You fall the way you lean.

Ham

Q: What did the cannibal's wife say when he brought home an actor?

A: Oh, good! Ham sandwiches.

Hands

Man: "I don't know what to do with my hands while I'm talking."

Woman: "Why don't you hold them over your mouth?"

Hang Gliding

After hang gliding all day, you might end up feeling soar all over.

Happiness

Happiness is not having what you want, but wanting what you have.

Hard-boiled Egg

Don't forget that people will judge you by your actions, not your intentions. You may have a heart of gold, but so does a hard-boiled egg.

Hardships

We don't fully realize the hardships that pioneers endured until we remember that day after day they plodded their way westward into the setting sun without sunglasses.

Harvard

Q: How many Harvard graduates does it take to screw in a light bulb?

A: Just one. He grabs the bulb and waits for the world to revolve around him.

Hate

Some people, by hating vice too much, come to love others too little.

He

Did you hear about the three He men?
He. He. He.

Headache

If you have a headache, thrust your head through a window, and the pane will disappear.

Hearse

People who drink and drive are putting the quart before the hearse.

Heimlich

Did you hear about the restaurant where all the waiters know the Heimlich maneuver? It's got a no-choking section.

Help

A man was attacked and left bleeding in a ditch. Two psychiatrists passed by, and one said to the other, "We must find the man who did this—he needs help."

Hereafter

The preacher visited me the other day. He said at my age, I should be thinking about the hereafter. I told him, "Oh, I do that all the time. No matter where I am—in the parlor, upstairs, in the kitchen, or down in the basement—I ask myself, 'Now, what am I here after?'"

Hermit

Did you hear about the hermit who got a traffic ticket? It was for recluse driving.

Hindsight

Hindsight is the reason they put all those three-way mirrors in department stores.

Hippo

Q: What do you call a very large animal that keeps taking pills?

A: A hippo-condriac.

Hold Your Hand

He: "May I hold your hand?"

She: "It isn't very heavy. I think I can manage it; thank you."

Hollywood

If idle minds are the devil's playground, then Hollywood must be his major amusement park.

Home

I come from a broken home. My kids have broken everything in it.

We have company in our house every day: the gas company, the mortgage company, and the electric company.

Homesick

"Can a person be in two places at the same time?"

"Certainly. Last week I was staying in Nebraska, and I was homesick the whole time."

Honeymoon

A woman in Colorado married so late in life that Medicare paid for her honeymoon.

You know the honeymoon is over when the husband has to wash and iron his own apron.

Horn of Plenty

You'll hear the horn of plenty when you are stuck in a traffic jam.

Horseradish

A student was learning about the different animals that provide food for people.

"If cows give us milk, chickens gives us eggs, and pigs give us bacon, what do horses give us?" asked the teacher.

"Horseradish!" replied one of the students.

Horse Sense

Horse sense is stable thinking coupled with the ability to say nay.

Host

You can always tell the host at a party. He's the one who keeps looking at his watch.

Hot Air

People who are always hitting the ceiling are apt to be full of hot air.

Hotels

I'm fed up with hotels that only hire inn-experienced people.

Hours

"Before I take this job, tell me, are the hours long?"
"No, only sixty minutes."

How Many Church Members Does It Take to Change a Light Bulb?

Charismatic: Only one. Hands are already in the air.

Pentecostal: Ten. One to change the bulb, and nine to pray against the spirit of darkness.

Presbyterian: None. Lights will go on and off at predestined times.

Roman Catholic: None. Candles only.

Baptist: At least fifteen. One to change the light bulb, and three committees to approve the change and decide who brings the potato salad and fried chicken.

Episcopalian: Three. One to call the electrician, one to mix the drinks, and one to talk about how much better the old one was.

Mormon: Five. One man to change the bulb, and four wives to tell him how to do it.

Unitarian: We choose not to make a statement either in favor of or against the need for a light bulb. However, if in your own journey you have found that light bulbs work for you, that is fine. You are invited to write a poem or compose a modern dance about your light bulb traditions, including candescent, fluorescent, three-way, long-life, and tinted—all of which are equally valid paths to luminescence.

Methodist: Undetermined. Whether your light is bright, dull, or completely out, you are loved. You can be a light bulb, turnip bulb, or tulip bulb. Church-wide lighting service is planned for Sunday. Bring bulb of your choice and a covered dish.

Nazarene: Six. One woman to replace the bulb, while five men review church lighting policy.

Lutheran: None. Lutherans don't believe in change.

Amish: What's a light bulb?

Husband

My husband doesn't know the meaning of fear. But then, there are many things he doesn't know.

A considerate husband is one who remembers to oil the lawnmower for his wife before he goes out to play golf.

Hypochondriac

A hypochondriac is someone who takes different pills than you do.

Hysterical

Husband: "I heard a great joke the other day. Did I tell it to you?"

Wife: "Was it funny?"

Husband: "It was hysterical."

Wife: "Then you didn't."

Ice Cream

Did you hear about the guy whose doctor told him to go on a liquid diet? He melted all his ice cream.

Idiot

"Would you marry an idiot for his money?"
"Is this a survey or a proposal?"

"I keep hearing the word *idiot*. I hope you're not referring to me."

"Don't be so conceited, as if there were no other idiots in the world!"

Impossible

If nothing is impossible, then how come you can't pick up a magazine without one of those subscription postcards falling out?

Nothing is impossible to the man who doesn't have to do it.

Inadequate

Two cows looked at a sign:

Pure Milk
Pasteurized
Homogenized
Vitamin D Added.

One cow said to the other, "Makes one feel a bit inadequate, doesn't it?"

Indians

When I was traveling out West, I met a large group of Indians who turned out to be one big Hopi family.

Inflation

If I get one more deduction on my take-home pay, I won't have a home to take the pay to.

Inflation has gotten so bad that you can put fifty dollars worth of groceries into your glove compartment.

Inflation has gotten so bad that your nest egg has turned out to be only chicken feed.

Inflation has gotten so bad that I heard a golfer yell, "Nine!"

If this isn't a recession, it must be the worst boom in history.

To help stem inflation and avoid pollution, just buy a new car and then don't drive it.

Ink
Joe: "What do you call frozen ink?"
Moe: "Iced ink."
Joe: "You're telling me!"

Insane
In all matters of opinion, our adversaries are insane.

Mark Twain

Insects

First man: "It's wonderful what some insects can do. A grasshopper can jump two hundred times its own length."

Second man: "That's nothing. I saw a tiny wasp raise a two hundred-pound man three feet off the ground."

Insider Trading

Q: What do they call an organ transplant?

A: Insider trading.

Insomnia

Lots of people build their dream house, and then get insomnia trying to figure out how to pay for it.

International Situation

Only one man in a million understands the international situation. Isn't it odd how you keep running into him at parties?

Inventor

Did you hear about the inventor of an automatic packaging machine? He made a bundle.

Invisible

Did you hear about the invisible man in the circus who married the invisible woman? Their kids weren't much to look at either.

IRS

The IRS sure knows how to take our money. You've really got to hand it to them.

Isms

Socialism: You give one of your two cows to your neighbor.

Communism: You give both of your cows to the government.

Capitalism: You sell one cow and buy a bull.

Jack and the Beanstalk

Do you remember the story of Jack and the beanstalk? Jack broke into the giant's house. That's breaking and entering. He stole the goose that lays the golden eggs. That's larceny. He chopped down the beanstalk and killed the giant. That's vandalism and murder.

Jack was small. The giant was big. Jack pulled a breaking and entering, larceny, vandalism, and murder, but came out the hero of the story. And the innocent giant became the villain.

Janitor

Did you hear about the janitor who asked his girlfriend to marry him? He swept her off her feet.

Job

The real reason congressmen are trying to get reelected is that they know they couldn't find another job in this economy.

Joke

He who laughs last is the guy who was intending to tell the same joke.

"Do you make up those jokes yourself?"
"Yep, out of my head."
"You must be."

Give me a sense of humor, Lord;
Give me the grace to see a joke.
To get some happiness from life,
And pass it on to other folk.

Junk

Behind every successful antique shop there's a junk store.

Junk is something you throw away three weeks before you need it.

Junk Mail

Whoever said you can't get something for nothing has obviously never received junk mail.

Jury

Juries must never be satisfied with their verdicts. They're always returning them to the judge.

Juvenile Delinquent

Did you hear about the juvenile delinquent from Beverly Hills? He's too young to drive, so he only steals cars with chauffeurs in them.

Kangaroo

They say a tired kangaroo is out of bounds.

Kick

"Have you ever tickled a mule?"

"No, I haven't."

"You should try it. You'll get a kick out of it."

Kleptomaniac

Our tests show you are a kleptomaniac.

What can I take for it, doc?

Labor Day

Q: When do most women give birth to their children?

A: On Labor Day.

Ladder

"Mom, I just knocked over the ladder that was leaning against the house."

"You'd better tell your dad about it."

"He knows. He was on the ladder at the time."

Las Vegas

When gambling became legal in Las Vegas, the mayor was heard to say that Las Vegas was now a bettor city.

Last Resort

The last resort is where you're stuck when you make your vacation plans late.

Laugh

If you think your boss never laughs, ask him for a raise.

Lawn Mower

"I heard you bought three lawn mowers."

"I had to. I have two neighbors."

Lawyer

I have a handshake deal with my lawyer. Every time I think of the deal, my hands shake!

Life

The real test in golf and in life is not keeping out of the rough, but getting out after we are in.

They say people are living longer now. They have to—who can afford to die?

Life is like a shower. One wrong turn, and you're in hot water.

Life is what passes you by while you're making other plans.

First man: "Life is like a fountain."

Second man: "Why is that?"

First man: "Okay, so life is not like a fountain."

Life Insurance

I heard you cancelled your life insurance.

Yes, I got tired of my wife telling everyone that I was worth more dead than alive.

Light Bulb

Thomas Edison had been staying up late every night for several weeks while trying to invent the electric light bulb. The operating principle was simple, but finding the right material for the filament proved daunting. Late one night, he finally discovered just the substance he needed and built the first light bulb. To his delight, it lit and burned steadily. Overjoyed, he picked it up and charged into the bedroom, where his wife was fast asleep.

"Darling, look! Look what I've invented!"

Mrs. Edison rolled over and said, "For heaven's sake, Tom, turn out the light and come to bed!"

Q: How many Californians does it take to change a light bulb?

A: Six. One to turn the bulb, one for support, and four to relate to the experience.

Lion

First hunter: "When I was in Africa, a lion ran across my path. I had no gun, so I threw a pail of water at him, and he ran away."

Second hunter: "I'll vouch for that. When I petted the lion's mane, it was still wet."

Listening

You know you're losing it when you start talking to yourself and even you aren't listening.

Listless

A sure cure for feeling listless is to write a list.

Little Red Riding Hood

The truth has surfaced about the case of Little Red Riding Hood. When the wolf was tried in circuit court, the judge dismissed the case because the wolf had not been informed of his rights. The ACLU provided an attorney for the wolf and the attorney entered a self-defense plea. The lawyer said that the wolf was only doing "what came naturally to him."

After the wolf was released, Little Red Riding Hood, her grandmother, and the woodchopper were arrested on charges of assault and battery with a deadly weapon. The three were sent to prison. Grandma's house was then turned into a national shrine. On dedication day, the nation's foremost activists were there. They spoke about human-rights violations against the wolf.

There wasn't a dry eye in the house.

Living

"Excuse me for living!"

"All right. But don't let it happen again."

Living Wage

What constitutes a living wage depends upon whether you are giving it or getting it.

Lot

Some folks have a lot on their mind—a vacant lot.

Love

Love is blind, and marriage is a real eye-opener.

In life, actions speak louder than words, but in love, the eyes do.

Love cures people—both the ones who give it and the ones who receive it.

If you would be loved, love and be lovable.

The way to love anything is to realize that it might be lost.

G.K. Chesterton

Love is softening of the hearteries.

Love is a fabric that never fades, no matter how often it is washed in the water of adversity and grief.

Love looks through a telescope; envy look through a microscope.

Love may not make the world go around, but it sure makes the trip worthwhile.

Faults are thick where love is thin.

Lulus

"Want to hear a couple of lulus?"
"Sure."
"Lulu...lulu."

Luxury

The difference between a luxury and a necessity is directly proportional to your inability to pay for it.

Mafia

Did you hear about the Mafia seafood restaurant? They call it Mobsters and Lobsters.

Man

There are three kinds of men who will never understand women: young men, middle-aged men, and old men.

Man's Best Friend

The real reason dogs are man's best friend is that they don't understand a word you're saying.

March

Can February March?
No, but April May.

Marriage

Marriage is like a midnight phone call. You get a ring, and then you wake up.

Matrimony isn't a word; it's a sentence.

Marriage is like horseradish—men praise it with tears in their eyes.

Marriage is like a violin—after the music stops, the strings are still attached.

The most dangerous year in married life is the first. Then follows the second, third, fourth, fifth…

The secret to a happy marriage is dinner out twice a week, and then a long, quiet walk home. My wife eats out on Tuesdays, and I eat out on Fridays.

We have been married for ten years, and I don't regret one day. The one day was July 15, 1967.

A wedding ring is a small gold band that cuts off your circulation.

First man: "I'll bet if I were married, I'd be the boss. I would tell my wife where to head in at."

Second man: "Yeah, and I suppose when you come to railroad tracks, you honk and the train just jumps out of the way."

They were married for better or for worse. He couldn't have done better, and she could have done worse.

First man: "Are you married?"

Second man: "No, I was hit by a truck."

Husband: "I wish you could make pies like my mother used to make."

Wife: "I wish you made the dough my father used to make."

Two persons can now live as cheaply as a family of ten used to.

First woman: "Who is your favorite author?"
Second woman: "My husband."
First woman: "What does he write?"
Second woman: "Checks."

Marriage Counselors

If love is a two-way street, then marriage counselors are highway maintenance.

Marriage License

Sign on the steps of a courthouse: This way for marriage licenses. Watch your step!

Sign on the door of a marriage license bureau: Out to lunch. Think it over.

Marriage Proposal

A marriage proposal is a speech usually made on the purr of the moment.

Match

"Have you any blue neckties to match my eyes?"
"No, but we have some soft hats to match your head."

Medium

A little man and a tall man decided to go into the

fortune-telling business. They advertised themselves as small medium and large.

Melodrama

Teacher: "Can someone tell me the difference between a drama and a melodrama?"

Student: "In a drama, the heroine merely throws the bad guy over. In a melodrama, she throws him over a cliff."

Memory

Every time you lend money to a friend, you damage his memory.

I have a memory like an elephant. In fact, elephants often consult me.

Mental Peak

Any parent will confirm that youngsters are at their mental peak between the ages of four and seventeen. At four they know all the questions. And at age seventeen they know all the answers.

Metal Illness

Are your kids listening to too much hard rock? It's a simple case of metal illness.

Million Dollars

"You look like a million dollars."

"But you have never seen a million dollars."

"That's what I mean. You look like something I have never seen before."

Mind

As soon as you open your mouth, your mind is on parade.

I like my bifocals,
    my dentures fit me fine.
My hearing aid is perfect,
    but how I miss my mind.

Miracle

A modern miracle would be a golden wedding anniversary in Hollywood.

Miraculous

Thanks to the miraculous strides made in medicine, people live longer...giving them the extra time they need to pay their medical bills.

Mistakes

Never put off until tomorrow what you can do today...unless you've already made your full quota of mistakes.

Mixed Up

Did you hear about the guy who crossed a bee with a lightning bug and got a bee that can work at night?

Did you hear about the guy who crossed a jellyfish with an electric eel and got current jelly?

Did you hear about the guy who got a job as a street peddler but went broke? Nobody wanted to buy a street.

Did you hear about the comedian who had a lot of funny lines? Too bad they are all in his face.

Did you hear about the man who invented a square bathtub so you won't get a ring?

Money

Looks can be deceiving. A dollar bill looks the same as it did ten years ago.

There are bigger things than money—bills.

Money isn't everything, but it does keep you in touch with your children.

Q: What do they call someone who is money mad?
A: A dough nut.

It's not wise to tell your kids the value of money anymore. You'll only discourage them.

Monogram

Is it true that people who start in the monogram business achieve initial success?

Monumental

Tombstone engraving is one of the oldest and kindest art forms in the world. Since epitaphs are, in essence, hand-carved letters of recommendation to God, they are almost invariably flattering. In the stonecutter's trade, the men who write those glowing tributes to the deceased are called "monumental liars."

Sam Levenson

Moon

Did you hear about the new restaurant that just opened up on the moon? Good food, but the atmosphere is terrible.

Moron

Have you noticed? Anyone driving faster than you is an idiot, and anyone driving slower than you is a moron.

Mortgage

Seventy percent of the earth is covered with water, and the other thirty percent is covered with mortgages.

Mother

The child had his mother's eyes, his mother's nose, and his mother's mouth. Which leaves his mother with a pretty blank expression.

Robert Benchley

Mountain Lion

Two men were out walking in the forest when suddenly a mountain lion began to pursue them. One of the men put on his tennis shoes.

First man: "You're crazy! You can't outrun a mountain lion."

Second man: "I don't have to outrun the lion. All I have to do is outrun you."

Mourning

Bill: "Why is Miss Ortman wearing black?"

Jill: "She's in mourning for her husband."

Bill: "Why? She never had a husband."

Jill: "That's why she mourns."

Movies

The movie was so bad that it curdled the butter on my popcorn.

Multiple Personality

Then there was the multiple-personality case who just wanted to be loved for himselves.

Mush

Did you hear about the fellow who stirred his mush with his fingers?

He wanted to feel his oats.

Music

When you are about 35 years old, something terrible always happens to music.

Today he is going to play like he never played before—
in tune.

Musical Insect

Q: What is another name for a musical insect?

A: Gnat King Cole.

Nails

"My brother is crazy. All day long he goes around biting
nails."

"What's so bad about that? Lots of people do that."

"My brother is a carpenter."

National Rifle Association

Did you know that members of the National Rifle
Association all wear short-sleeved shirts? They believe that it
is their right to bare arms.

Natural Ingredients

A father was reading a bedtime story to his daughter:

"No, I don't know whether the porridge was made with
all-natural ingredients. Now may I continue?"

Neurosis

A neurosis is when you realize that life is a great journey,
and you're sure you've lost your boarding pass.

New Age

Did you hear about the New Age church in California? It
has three commandments and six suggestions.

Newly Married Husband

"I've eaten so much frozen food that I have the only tonsils in town that are chapped."

Ninety

Did you hear about the two ninety-year-olds who got married? They never argue. They can't hear each other.

Nine Words Women Use

1. *Fine:* This is the word women use to end an argument when they are right and you need to shut up.

2. *Five minutes:* If she is getting dressed, this means a half an hour. Five minutes is only five minutes when you have just been given five more minutes to watch the game before helping around the house.

3. *Nothing:* This is the calm before the storm. This means something, and you should be on your toes. Arguments that begin with *nothing* usually end in "Fine!"

4. *Go Ahead:* This is a dare, *not* permission. Don't do it!

5. *Loud Sigh:* This is actually a word, but is a nonverbal statement often misunderstood by men. A loud sigh means she thinks you are an idiot and wonders why she is wasting her time standing there and arguing with you about nothing. (Refer back to number 3 for the meaning of nothing.)

6. *That's okay:* This is one of the most dangerous statements a woman can make to a man. "That's okay" means she wants to think long and hard before deciding how and when you will pay for your mistake.

7. *Thanks:* When a woman is thanking you, do not question her or faint. Just say, "You're welcome."

8. *Whatever:* Is a woman's way of saying shut up...*now!*

9. *Don't worry about it; I got it:* This is another dangerous statement. This is what she says after she has told a man to do something several times, but she is now doing it herself. This will later result in a man asking, "What's wrong?" For the woman's response to the man, refer to number 3.

Noise

"A noise woke me up this morning."
"What was it?"
"I think it was the crack of dawn."

Note

A teacher received a note from a mother to excuse her child from school:

> Please excuse Christy from being absent. She has a viral infection. I am having her shot tonight.

Nuts

Shake any family tree, and you're bound to get a few nuts.

"You must be forty-four years old."
"How did you know?"
"My brother is twenty-two, and he's half nuts."

Q: What is the best housewarming gift for a husband and wife who are both psychiatrists?

A: An assortment of nuts.

Obstetrician

An obstetrician is a doctor who makes money in the stork market.

Offer

"Today is my wife's birthday."
"What are you getting for her?"
"Make me an offer."

Off His Rocker

The results are in from a new experiment at mental hospitals. They find that people who sit in rocking chairs all day are seldom off their rockers.

Oil Drilling

They say that oil drilling is a boring profession.

Old Age

He's so old that when he orders a three-minute egg, they ask for the money up front.

I've reached the age at which a good day is one on which, when you get up, nothing hurts.

As we grow older, our bodies get shorter and our anec-dotes longer.

He's so old that his blood type has been discontinued.

My, my—sixty-five years old. I guess this marks the first day of the rest of our savings.

She was over a hundred years of age. She didn't have wrinkles; she had pleats.

He was so old that when he went to school they didn't have history.

I'm beginning to appreciate the value of naps. They are wonderful. Sometimes I even take a nap to get ready for bed.

One of the first signs of getting old is when your head makes dates your body can't keep.

Old teachers never die. They just lose their principals.

Old principals never die. They just lose their faculties.

Old students never die. They just lose their class.

"Do you think I look old?"
"No, indeed; you're not half as old as you look."

There are four advantages to getting old and forgetful: One, you meet new friends every day. Two, every joke you hear is new. Three, you can hide your own Easter eggs. And I forget the fourth one.

The principal objection to old age is there's no future in it.

Old-fashioned
The old-fashioned family doctor is disappearing, and so is the old-fashioned family.

Old Pirates
Old pirates never die. They just become presidents of savings and loan companies.

One Wish
There were three men marooned on an island. Two were preachers, and one was a college president. After they were

marooned there for several weeks, a bottle floated up, and one of them went and got it.

He said, "Do you reckon there could be…?"

One of the others said, "Well, there might be…"

One of them pulled the cork out of the bottle, rubbed it, and a genie came out. He said, "I can grant each of you one wish. So what do you want?"

One of the ministers said, "You know, I miss my congregation so much, I wish I was back there with them." And he was gone!

The other preacher said, "I miss my wife and family so much, I wish I was back there with them." And poof—he was gone too.

The genie looked at the college president and said, "I can grant you a wish as well. What do you want?"

He thought for a minute, then said, "You know, I'm just not used to making a decision on my own. I wish those other two fellows were back here to help me."

Ostrich

An ostrich that keeps its head in the sand too long gets burned in the end.

Over the Hill

Silver in their hair,
Gold in their teeth,
Stones in their kidneys,
Lead in their feet, and
Gas in their stomachs.

When you're over the hill, your speed picks up.

Being over the hill is a lot better than being under it.

The worst part about being over the hill is you don't recall ever being on top of it.

Pain Threshold
Q: What is the pain threshold?

A: The doorway to the dentist's office.

Pane
People find that living in glass houses is a real pane.

Panic
A man was being tried for murder. He was in a panic that he might be convicted for capital punishment. With that thought in mind, he found one of the elderly jurors and bribed him with all of his life savings. "Please help me to get a manslaughter verdict," he requested.

The trial went on for days and days. Finally the verdict was reached. The jury gave him manslaughter. With tears of gratitude, the man thanked the juror before he was sent to prison.

"How did you do it?" he asked.

"It was not easy," said the elderly juror. "They all wanted to acquit you."

Parachute

I heard that someone with a parachute jumped off the Eiffel Tower and ended up in the river below. I think the man was in Seine.

Paranoia

Friday afternoon I was walking home from school and I watched some builders working on a new house. And the guy hammering on the roof called me a paranoid little weirdo. In Morse code.

Q: How many paranoid schizophrenics does it take to screw in a light bulb?

A: Who wants to know?

It's hard to be nice to some paranoid schizophrenics—even if they live in your body.

What's so awful about being a paranoid? Two noids are better than one.

I'm very insecure. I get depressed when I find out the people I hate don't like me.

I'm kind of paranoid, too. I often think the car in front of me is following me the long way around.

🍵   🍵   🍵

I wanted to go to the Paranoids Anonymous meeting, but they wouldn't tell me where it was.

Parasites

When we visited Europe, we spent a good deal of time in Paris. We enjoyed looking at all of the parasites.

Parking Place

Have you ever noticed that empty parking spaces are always on the other side of the street? So you go around the block, only to find that the empty parking spaces are still on the other side of the street.

Parrot

Q: What do you call a parrot wearing a raincoat?

A: Polly unsaturated.

Passport

"I take the worst possible view of everyone."

"Oh, you must be a pessimist."

"No, I'm a passport photographer."

Patience

A doctor's waiting room is where the patients test their patience.

Patronage

Shopkeeper: "Thank you, Mr. Poure, for your patronage. I wish I had twenty customers like you."

Mr. Poure: "That surprises me. I protest every bill you send, and never pay you on time."

Shopkeeper: "I'd still wish I had twenty customers like you. The problem is, I have two hundred."

Paycheck

"Where's my paycheck?" asked the clerk of the paymaster in the big plant.

The cashier explained, "Well, after deducting withholding tax, state income tax, city tax, Social Security, retirement fund, unemployment insurance, hospitalization, dental insurance, group life insurance, and your donation to the company welfare fund, you owe us fourteen dollars and twenty-five cents."

Joey Adams

Peace

Our pastor's sermons are like the peace of God. They surpass all understanding.

Sam Levenson

Penny

"A penny for your thoughts" is something you'll never hear a psychiatrist say.

People

There are three kinds of people in this world: those who make things happen, those who watch things happen, and those who don't know what's happening.

Perks

Did you hear about the college graduate who got a job with a coffee company? He got a very good salary with lots of perks.

Per Pound

A woman walked into a butcher shop and asked the price of a pound of tenderloin.

Butcher: "It's thirteen dollars a pound."

Woman: "Are you sure? That can't be!"

Butcher: "Look at the sign, lady. It says thirteen dollars a pound."

Woman: "That seems higher than what other butchers in the area charge."

Butcher: "They're probably giving you a poorer cut of beef."

Woman: "No, the butcher across the street has it priced at nine dollars a pound."

Butcher: "Well, then, why don't you go buy your meat there?"

Woman: "Because he is all out of tenderloin."

Butcher: "When I'm all out of tenderloin, I sell it for seven dollars a pound."

Perseverance

Perseverance is not a long race; it is many short races one after another.

Perspective

Dear Mother and Dad,

Since I left for college, I've been remiss in writing, and I'm sorry for my thoughtlessness in not having written yet. I will bring you up to date now, but before you read on, please sit down. You are not to read any further unless you are sitting down.

I am getting along pretty well now. The skull fracture and concussion I got when I jumped out the window of my dormitory, which caught fire shortly after my arrival here, is pretty well healed now. I spent only two weeks in the hospital, and now my eyesight is almost back to normal and I get those sickening headaches only once a day.

Fortunately, the fire in the dormitory and my jump were witnessed by an attendant at the gas station near the dorm, and he was the one who called the fire department and the ambulance. He also visited me in the hospital. Because the dormitory had burned down and I had nowhere to live, he kindly invited me to share his apartment with him. It's really a basement room, but it's kind of cute.

He is a fine boy, and we have fallen deeply in love and are planning on getting married in the near future. We haven't set an exact date yet, but it will be before my pregnancy begins to show. Yes, Mother and Dad, I am pregnant. I know how much you are looking forward to being grandparents, and I know you will welcome the baby into your home and give it the same love and devotion and tender care you gave me when I was a child.

The reason for the delay in our marriage is that my boyfriend is trying to get a job. He is very sweet and kind, but not terribly bright, nor educated, nor ambitious.

Now that I have brought you up to date, I want to tell you that there was no fire, and I was not injured. I did not go to the hospital. I am not pregnant. I am not engaged. There is no boyfriend in my life. However, I am getting a D in history and an F in chemistry, and I wanted you to see those marks in proper perspective.

Your loving daughter

Pessimist

A pessimist is someone who looks at life through woes-colored glasses.

A pessimist is someone who builds dungeons in the air.

Pesticides

Ashes to ashes and dust to dust,
If the smog doesn't get you, then pesticides must.

Pew

Did you hear about the miner in California who worked for two weeks without taking a bath and then discovered gold? He yelled, "Eureka!" His partner who worked with him replied, "You don't smell so good yourself!"

Philosophy

You're young only once, but you can be immature all your life.

Jumping to conclusions is not nearly as good an exercise as digging for the facts.

When I was young, I was told to listen to my elders. Now I'm an elder, and I'm told to listen to the young folk. Somehow I missed life along the way.

Phobias

Q: What do you call a doctor who specializes in phobias?

A: An Afraidan psychologist.

Pierced

If you really want your ears pierced, try listening to heavy metal music.

Pig

From a rural district in England comes the story of a driver of a small sedan braking hastily as the tweedy mistress of the largest estate thereabouts came hurtling around a sharp bend in the narrow road in her large Rolls Royce. Before the driver of the sedan could say a word, she shouted, "Pig!" and drove on.

"Fat old cow!" he cried after her in retaliation. Then he drove around the bend...and crashed head-on into the biggest pig he'd ever seen.

Bennett Cerf

Pigeon

Did you hear about the man who harnessed a large flock of pigeons to his bicycle? He wanted to experiment with being pigeon towed.

Place in the Sun

If you want a place in the sun, you have to expect some blisters.

Plants

"Why does your wife always wear a flower in her hair?"
"She wants to show who wears the plants in the family."

Plastic Surgeon

Q: What do they call a plastic surgeon?

A: A cosmedic.

Podiatrist

Podiatrists have got a real foothold in the medical profession.

First man: "I just found out that there are now two podiatrists in town."

Second man: "They must be arch rivals."

Poison Ivy

Did you hear about the guy who crossed poison ivy with a four-leaf clover and got a rash of good luck?

Politician

A politician is someone who shakes your hand before the election and your confidence after.

Q: Why are politicians like polkas?

A: They have different names, but they all sound alike.

Christopher Columbus was the world's first politician. He didn't know where he was going. He didn't know where he was when he got there. And he did it all on somebody else's money.

Politics

Politics is the art of looking for trouble, finding it every-where, diagnosing it incorrectly, and applying the wrong remedies.

Groucho Marx

Q: What's the difference between baseball and politics?

A: In baseball, you're out if you're caught stealing.

Q: How many presidents does it take to change a light bulb?

A: They'll only promise change.

Pollution

I remember when "Smoke Gets in Your Eyes" was a song and not a weather report.

Spring must be here. The smog is turning green.

Pollution has become so bad, we now pray, "Give us this day our daily breath!"

If this country's pollution gets any worse, we'll soon be saying, "One nation, invisible…"

Porcupine

A lovelorn porcupine was taking an evening stroll when he bumped into a cactus. "Is that you, sweetheart?" he asked tenderly.

Pork Barrels

Maybe we wouldn't have to worry so much about congressional pork barrels if there weren't so many swine in Washington.

These days the ship of state seems to carry only one cargo: pork barrels.

Postage

Postage is so high now, every time you mail a get well card you get sick.

Pam: "Why was your letter so damp?"

Melba: "Postage dew, I guess."

Post Office

If you're tired of living life in the fast lane, get a job at the post office.

Poverty

Poverty is what we try to conceal while we're going through it, and then brag about in our memoirs when we're past it.

I used to think I was poor. Then they told me I wasn't poor, I was needy. Then they told me it was self-defeating to think of myself as needy. I was deprived. (Oh, not deprived but rather, underprivileged.) Then they told me that under-privileged was overused. I was disadvantaged. I still don't have a dime. But I have a great vocabulary.

Jules Feiffer

Practice

If you think practice makes perfect, you don't have a child taking piano lessons.

Preacher

Did you hear about the preacher who complained that he was working himself to death for heaven's sake?

Press Agent

Have you ever noticed that when you make a total fool of yourself, everyone wants to be your press agent?

Principal

I always liked school. It was the principal of the thing I hated.

Psychiatrist

Psychiatrist: "Tell me, Madam, does your son have a behavior problem?"

Mother: "I don't know. He has never behaved."

Teacher: "Can someone tell me why it is believed that the people who live in big cities are not as smart as those who live in smaller towns?"

Student: "That's where the population is the most dense."

Did you hear about the psychiatrist who gave his son a set of mental blocks for Christmas?

Q: How many psychiatrists does it take to change a light bulb?

A: One. But the light bulb has to really want to change.

Never tell a psychiatrist you're a schizophrenic. He'll charge you double.

He was so normal that it took the psychiatrist a long time to figure out what was wrong with him.

A psychiatrist is someone who asks you a lot of expensive questions that your spouse asks you for free.

Psychiatrist to IRS official: "Nonsense, the whole world isn't against you. Maybe all the people in the United States, but certainly not the whole world."

Psychiatrists tell us that girls tend to marry men who are like their fathers. Now we know why mothers cry at weddings.

A psychiatrist is a man who will listen to you as long as you don't make sense.

Be a good psychiatrist, and all the world will beat a psychopath to your door.

I've been told that the psychiatrist's motto is, "You're only Jung once, but that's nothing to be a Freud of."

Psychiatry

Q: What do they do at psychiatry school?

A: They learn the nuts and bolts of nuts.

Psychoanalysis

Q: How many psychoanalysts does it take to screw in a light bulb?

A: How many do you think it takes?

Pun

The pun is mightier than the sword.

Punishment

Did you hear about the man who told so many puns that they put him to death? Someone called it capital *pun*ishment.

Pupils

We know a principal who will not hire cross-eyed teachers because they can't control their pupils.

Purse

"Say, honey, could you fix my purse?"

"Sure. What's wrong with it?"

"It's empty."

Quaker

Asked to tell his class something about the Quakers, the little boy replied, "The Quakers are very meek, quiet people who never fight or answer back. I think my father is a Quaker. Not my mother."

Sam Levenson

Quarterbacks

Quarterbacks never retire; they just pass away.

Running backs never retire; they just get run down.

Questions

It used to be that growing up meant getting all your questions answered. Now it means getting all your answers questioned.

Quicksand

Have you heard the joke about quicksand? It takes a long time to sink in.

Ready

"Aren't you ready yet?"

"I've been telling you for the last hour that I would be ready in a minute!"

Reality

Reality is the only obstacle to happiness.

Infatuation is when you think that he's as sexy as Robert Redford, as smart as Henry Kissinger, as noble as Ralph Nader, as funny as Woody Allen, and as athletic as Jimmy Connors. Love is when you realize that he's as sexy as Woody Allen, as smart as Jimmy Connors, as funny as Ralph Nader, as athletic as Henry Kissinger, and nothing like Robert Redford—but you'll take him anyway.

Judith Viorst

Really Stinks

They ought to expand the movie-rating system to include RS for Really Stinks.

Realtor

A realtor is someone who's always putting people in their place.

Recess

I've been told that the motto for grade-school teachers is "Nothing succeeds like recess."

Recliner

They say that a recliner is a vinyl resting place.

Recovery Rooms

Hospitals ought to put their recovery rooms right next to the cashier's office.

Redneck Ten Commandments

1. Just one God.
2. Put nothin' before God.
3. Watch yer mouth.
4. Git yourself to Sunday meeting.
5. Honor yer Ma and Pa.
6. No killin'.
7. No foolin' around with another fellow's gal.
8. Don' take what ain't yers.
9. No tellin' tales or gossipin'.
10. Don't be hankerin' for yer buddy's stuff.

Redundant

Help stamp out and abolish redundancy!

Reject

A relative of mine willed his body to science. Science is contesting the will.

Reminisce

People who like to reminisce live life in the past lane.

Repeat

"Repetition is very important," said the professor. "Repeat a word twenty-five times, and it will be yours for life."

In the back of the classroom, a coed closed her eyes and said, "Jacob, Jacob, Jacob..."

Report Card

A little learning is a dangerous thing. Ask any child who has brought home a bad report card.

Restaurant

I like a dimly lit restaurant. By the time the waiter finds the 25-cent tip, I'm gone.

Review

Some people can read you like a book review.

Rheumatism

A candidate for the Senate was waxing pretty eloquent on the evils of leftist politics to a rural audience. He shouted at the top of his lungs, "We've got to get rid of all these threats to our way of life. I mean bolshevism, socialism, communism..."

A old farmer interrupted, "While you're at it, why don't you get rid of rheumatism, too?"

Right Mind

If the right half of the brain controls the left side of the body, and the left half of the brain controls the right side of the body, does that mean that left-handed people are the only ones in their right mind?

Ring

Love has been described as a five-ring circus: First comes the telephone ring, then the engagement ring, then the wedding ring, then the teething ring, and after that the suffer-ring.

Robbery

Did you hear about the man who robbed a music store and escaped with the lute?

Rumors

Rumors spread like butter. Ever try to unspread butter?

Rush Hour

Why do they call it rush hour when nothing moves?

Saddled

The reason most folks don't show any horse sense is that they don't want to be saddled with responsibility.

Safari

"I'm going on a safari to Africa."
"Drop us a lion now and then."
"Sounds fishy to me!"

Santa

A man goes through three stages: First, he believes in Santa. Then he does not believe in Santa. Then finally, he is Santa.

Schizophrenic

At least a schizophrenic knows how the other half lives.

School

A first grader came home from school one day with a zero marked on his paper.

His mother exclaimed, "Ryan, why did you get that zero?"

Ryan responded, "That's no zero, mommy. The teacher ran out of stars and she gave me a moon."

I went to correspondence school. They threw me out for playing hooky...I sent them an empty envelope.

My school was so tough that when the kids had their school pictures taken, one shot was taken from the front and another shot was taken from the side.

Seashell

I don't want to say that my life is difficult, but every time I put a seashell to my ear, I get a busy signal.

Secretary

My wife doesn't care what my secretary looks like, just as long as he's efficient.

Self-help

I went to a bookstore and asked the woman behind the counter where the self-help section was. She said, "If I told you, that would defeat the whole purpose."

Senile

Q: What do they call tourists in Egypt?

A: Senile people.

Shady

Did you hear about the man who made millions in the lamp manufacturing business? He kept meeting a lot of shady characters.

Ship of State

The ship of state would be better off if there weren't so many pirates on board.

Shocking

"Have you ever touched a live wire?"

"No, but I've heard it's a shocking experience."

Short

My wife is a real master at making a long story short—she keeps interrupting me.

Shovel

The best way to get your teenager to shovel the snow in the driveway is to tell him he can use the car.

Show Me

Show me a burned-out post office, and I'll show you a case of blackmail.

Show me a fowl with an artificial leg, and I'll show you a lame duck.

Show me a home where the buffalo roams and the deer and the antelope play, and I'll show you a very messy house.

Show me a part-time magician, and I'll show you an abracadabbler.

Show me a singing beetle, and I'll show you a humbug.

Show me a wife and mother-in-law in the backseat of a car, and I'll show you a steering committee.

Show me an arsonist, and I'll show you a man with a burning desire.

Show me where Stalin is buried, and I'll show you a Communist plot.

Show me a good loser, and I'll show you a man who is playing golf with his boss.

Show me a man convicted of two crimes, and I'll show you a compound sentence.

Show me a person who loves concerts, and I'll show you a symphomaniac.

Show me a man who smiles when everything goes wrong, and I'll show you a repairman.

Show me a man who understands women, and I'll show you a man in for a big surprise.

Shrink Wrap
Q: What do they call the coat that a psychiatrist wears?
A: A shrink wrap.

Shrubs
When I spend all day trimming the shrubs around our house, I feel bushed.

Sick

Sickness comes in four stages—ill, pill, bill, and will.

Does he miss church service?
　　He *may* be sick.
Does he miss work?
　　He *probably* is sick.
Does he miss his favorite sport or amusement?
　　He *is* really sick!

Signs of the Time

Sign in dentist's office:

> Be true to your teeth
> or they will be false to you.

Teeth Extracted by Latest Methodists

Sign outside a cabinet shop:

> We are professional counter fitters.

Sign placed by a tennis pro offering discounts:

> First come, first serve.

Sign at a junkyard:

> Our Business Is Picking Up

Sign at a restaurant:
> Fire Sale! Eat here or we'll get fired.

Sign on the back of a bus:
> Approach with care.
> Driver under the influence of children.

Sign at a travel agency:
> Go away!

Sign at the edge of an African desert:
> Last chance to fill up.
> The next two stations are mirages.

Sign at a restaurant:
> Delightful tongue sandwiches.
> They speak for themselves.

Sign outside a motel:
> Inn mates wanted.

Sign at a beauty salon:
> Let us curl up and dye for you!

Sign at a park lawn:
Your feet are killing me!

Sign on a door at a nuclear power plant:
Gone Fission

Sign at a jail:
If you don't like it here, stay out!

Sign at a ski resort:
There's no business like snow business.

Sign at an undertaker's:
Drive with care.
Don't insist on your rites.

Sign at a church:
Come in now and get your faith lifted.

If absence makes the heart grow fonder,
an awful lot of people love our church.

Sign at a restaurant:
>Don't stand outside and look miserable.
>Come inside and be fed up.

Sign in a newspaper:
>Happy home wanted for lively but good-tempered dog.
>Will eat anything, loves children.

Sign at a maternity store:
>Expansion sale!

Sign in a clothing store:
>Wonderful bargains for men
>with 16 and 17 necks.

Sign in a restaurant window:
>Eat here and you'll never eat anyplace else again.

Silence

I have noticed that nothing I have never said ever did me any harm.

Calvin Coolidge

Silly Thoughts

If a man from Great Neck is a Great Necker, is a man from Baltimore a Baltimoron?

If a meat market sells meat, what do you buy at a flea-market?

If a painter paints, does a waiter wait?

If a pressure cooker cooks pressure, does a meat loaf?

If a rubber band stretches, will a bed spread?

If a snowball is made from snow, what are snow tires made of?

If a weightlifter lifts weights, does a shoplifter lift shops?

If a young child is a baby, is a young doctor a baby doctor?

If dog food is for dogs, is chicken soup for chickens?

If ignorance is bliss, why aren't more people happy?

If it is a small world, why does it cost so much to run it?

If it takes an apple a day to keep the doctor away, what does it take to get rid of a nurse?

If money doesn't grow on trees, why do banks have so many branches?

If olive oil comes from olives, where does baby oil come from?

If a temple were built in Shirley, Long Island, would they call it Shirley Temple?

If we get honey from honeybees, do we get butter from butterflies?

If you feed sheep ironized yeast, will you get steel wool?

If you filled your waterbed with root beer, would you get a foam mattress?

Silver Lining

I've been hunting for the silver lining for more than half a century. Why is it always easier to find in someone else's cloud?

Sir Lancelot

I was told that Sir Lancelot once had a very frightening dream. It was a real knight-mare.

Six Phases of a Project

1. Enthusiasm
2. Disillusionment
3. Panic and hysteria
4. Search for the guilty
5. Punishment of the innocent
6. Praise and honor for the nonparticipants

Sleep

Why do people who snore always fall asleep first?

Sleep Deprivation

Have you heard about the new sleep deprivation experiment? It's called parenting.

Sleeping Bag

They call a sleeping bag a nap sack.

Sleeves

When you roll up your sleeves, you seldom lose your shirt.

Smart

Smart Son: "Dad, I just siphoned a couple of gallons of gas out of your car and put them in my car. It's okay, isn't it?"

Smarter Father: "Sure, it's okay, son. I bought that gas with your allowance for next week. So run along and have a good time."

Smooth Sea

A smooth sea never made a skillful mariner.

Socialized Medicine

Socialized medicine is when people sit around the table at a bridge party and talk about their operations.

Soft Spot

She: "I always had a soft spot in my heart for you."

He: "Then let's get married."

She: "I said a soft spot in my heart, not my head."

Some People

Some people are like rocking chairs: a lot of action, but no progress.

Some people don't have much to say. The only trouble is that you have to wait too long to find that out.

Some people drive a car as if they were rehearsing for an accident.

Some people only have two faults: what they do, and what they say.

Some people who think they have an open mind actually have a hole in their head.

Some people work up a steam, and some only generate a fog.

Speculation

"There are two times in a man's life when he shouldn't speculate: When he can't afford it, and when he can."

Mark Twain

Speed of Light

The worst part about the speed of light is it makes the mornings come awfully early.

Spelling Bee

It was a terrible day. First I got tonsillitis, followed by appendicitis, and then pneumonia. After that I got rheumatism. And on top of all that, they gave me hypodermics and inoculations. I thought I would never get through the spelling bee.

Spoil

The best way to spoil a good discussion is to include someone who knows what he's talking about.

Spoiled

"Your sister is spoiled, isn't she?"

"No, that's just the perfume she's wearing."

Stairs

"Do these stairs take me to the second floor?"

"No, you'll have to walk."

Staph

They call a doctors' conference on infection a staph meeting.

Statistician

Old statisticians never die; they just know when their number is up.

Statue

"Why do you have a statue under the kitchen sink?"

"Shh! That's the plumber."

Steam Shovel

"I just saw a steam shovel."

"Don't tell me that! Nobody can shovel steam."

Steering Committee

Q: What is a steering committee?

A: It's when you have two backseat drivers.

Stew

Customer: "Is there stew on the menu today, waiter?"

Waiter: "No, sir. I wiped it off."

Stitch

A stitch in time saves you from jogging any further, if the stitch is in your side.

Stockbroker

A stockbroker is a modern-day magician. He knows how to make your money disappear.

Story

An old-timer is someone who can remember every detail of his life story, but can't remember how many times he's told it to the same person.

Strange Occupations

I would like to meet an airplane spotter.

I would like to meet an ambulance stretcher.

I would like to meet an animal cracker.

I would like to meet an ant eater.

I would like to meet a bargain counter.

I would like to meet a bedroom dresser.

I would like to meet a belly dancer.

I would like to meet a book worm.

I would like to meet a card shark.

I would like to meet a chain smoker.

I would like to meet a clock puncher.

I would like to meet a crop duster.

I would like to meet a dumb waiter.

I would like to meet a dust collector.

I would like to meet an ear puller.

I would like to meet an eye dropper.

I would like to meet a face lifter.

I would like to meet a feather duster.

I would like to meet a fire cracker.

I would like to meet a fly catcher.

I would like to meet a glass blower.

I would like to meet a gum wrapper.

I would like to meet a hair teaser.

I would like to meet an ice breaker.

I would like to meet a jaw breaker.

I would like to meet a lazy Susan.

I would like to meet a litter bug.

I would like to meet a loan shark.

I would like to meet a name dropper.

I would like to meet a road hog.

I would like to meet a penny pincher.

I would like to meet a pinch hitter.

I would like to meet a pipe cleaner.

I would like to meet a pot holder.

I would like to meet a salt shaker.

I would like to meet a shoulder guard.

I would like to meet a sky scraper.

I would like to meet a tongue depressor.

I would like to meet a tooth picker.

I would like to meet a weight watcher.

I would like to meet a West Pointer.

I would like to meet a wise cracker.

Stupid

Just when you think you know the meaning of the word *stupid*, someone comes along and redefines it.

Success

There are seven ways to elude success:

1. Don't look—you might see.
2. Don't listen—you might hear.
3. Don't think—you might learn.
4. Don't make decisions—they might be wrong.
5. Don't walk—you might stumble.
6. Don't run—you might fall.
7. Don't live—you might die.

There's no secret about success. Did you ever know a successful man who didn't tell you all about it?

All my life I've said I wanted to be someone. I can see now that I should have been more specific.

Success is relative. The more success, the more relatives.

If you don't know the price of success, the Internal Revenue Service will.

If at first you don't succeed, at least you'll get lots of free advice on how to.

Successful Marriage

A successful marriage is based on the ability to pretend you don't know what your spouse is thinking.

Sue

Did you hear about the personal injury lawyer who named his daughter Sue?

Suffering

Why do you sing with your eyes closed?
I hate to see people suffer.

Suit

Clothes don't make the man, but a good suit makes a lawyer.

Summer Camp

The person who invented summer camp ought to get the Nobel Peace Prize.

Sunday Driving

On Sunday, many people hear the crawl of the open road.

Sunday School

Teacher: "Does anyone know who lived in the Garden of Eden?"

Student: "It was the Adams Family."

Sunrise

"I can lie in bed in the morning and watch the sun rise."

"That's nothing. I can sit in the living room and see the kitchen sink."

Support

Life is a big struggle to support a wife, children, and the government at the same time.

Surprise

Q: How many mystery writers does it take to screw in a light bulb?

A: Two. One to screw it almost all the way in, and the other to give it a surprising twist at the end.

I couldn't stand it any longer. I finally washed all the makeup off my teenage daughter's face and pushed back all of her hair. And do you know what? I've been raising somebody else's kid!

Surprise Me

A son spoke to his elderly father who was dying.

Son: "Where do you want to be buried? At Forest Lawn, or in Atlanta, Georgia?"

Father: "Surprise me."

Take-out

Husband: "What's for supper?"

Wife: "Take-out."

Husband: "What kind of take-out?"

Wife: "Me."

Talking to Yourself

There's nothing wrong with talking to yourself. Lots of people do it; they're called parents.

It's all right if you talk to yourself. It's also okay if you answer yourself. It's when you start disagreeing with your answers that you've got a problem.

Tantrum

When painters throw a fit, it is called a tempera tantrum.

Tapeworm

Q: What do you get when you cross a porcupine with a tapeworm?

A: Ten feet of barbed wire.

Taxes

It is hard to believe that America was founded to avoid taxes.

Things could be worse. What if the tax office were to start charging for the tax forms?

I'm putting all my money in taxes—it's the only thing sure to go up this year.

Taxidermist

The difference between a taxidermist and a tax collector is that the taxidermist leaves the hide.

A taxidermist is a skin doctor for cabbies.

Teacher

My history teacher is so old, she doesn't teach history—she remembers it.

Teaching

Teaching may not pay much, but at least it's a job with class.

Technology

It is reported that a high-level computer manufacturer compared the computer industry with the auto industry. He said, "If General Motors had kept up with technology like the computer industry has, we would all be driving twenty-five-dollar cars that got a thousand miles to the gallon."

In response, the motor company issued a press release:

If General Motors had developed technology like the computer companies, we all would be driving cars with following characteristics:

1. For no reason whatsoever, your car would crash… twice a day.

2. Every time they repainted the lines in the road, you would have to buy a new car.

3. Occasionally your car would die on the freeway for no reason. You would have to pull to the side of the road, close all of the windows, shut off the car, restart it, and reopen the windows before you could continue. For some reason, you would simply accept this.

4. Occasionally, executing a maneuver such as a left turn would cause your car to shut down and refuse to restart, in which case you would have to reinstall the engine.

5. The car would be powered by the sun, it would be reliable, it would go five times as fast, and it would be twice as easy to drive—but it would run on only five percent of the roads.

6. The oil, water temperature, and alternator warning lights would all be replaced by a single: "This car has performed an illegal operation" warning light.

7. The airbag system would ask, "Are you sure?" before deploying.

8. Occasionally, for no reason whatsoever, your car would lock you out and refuse to let you in until you simultaneously lifted the door handle, turned the key, and grabbed hold of the radio antenna.

9. Every time a new car was introduced, car buyers would have to learn how to drive all over again, because none of the controls would operate in the same manner as the old car.

10. You would have to press the *Start* button to turn off the engine.

11. If you had any problems with your new car of the future, you could call customer service in some foreign country and be instructed, in some foreign language, how to fix your car by yourself.

Teens

Your teen years were the last stage in your life when you were happy to hear that the phone was for you.

Teens are at an awkward stage in life. They know how to make phone calls, but not how to end them.

Teeth

He can't help being stupid. He has cavities in his wisdom teeth.

Television

A recent poll reported that the more intelligent a person is, the less he watches television. Personally, I think that's backward: The more a person watches television, the less intelligent he becomes.

Say, shall we watch the six o'clock news and get indigestion, or wait for the eleven o'clock news and get insomnia?

Television permits you to be entertained in your living room by characters you wouldn't ordinarily allow in your home.

Have you ever noticed that families on TV shows never watch television?

We've finally found the educational channel on our TV set. It's marked *Off*.

Temper Tantrum

If a four-year-old becomes uncontrollable and starts throwing things, it's called a temper tantrum. When a 20-year-old does it, it's called a justified, politically oriented demonstration against the establishment.

Temptation

Lots of people can resist temptation...some even for as long as 15 minutes.

Opportunity knocks, but temptation kicks the door down. Opportunity knocks only once; temptation leans on the doorbell.

Tennessee Medical Terminology

Artery	The study of fine paintings
Barium	What to do when CPR fails
Benign	What you be after you be eight
Caesarean section	A district in Rome
Colic	A sheep dog
Congenital	Friendly
Dilate	Live long
Fester	Quicker
GI series	Baseball games between teams of soldiers
Hangnail	A coat hook
Medical staff	A doctor's cane
Minor operation	Coal digging
Morbid	A higher offer
Nitrate	Lower than the day rate
Node	Was aware of
Organic	Church musician
Outpatient	A person who has fainted
Postoperative	A letter carrier
Protein	In favor of young people
Secretion	Hiding anything

Serology	A study of English knighthood
Tablet	A small table
Tumor	An extra pair
Urine	Opposite of "You're out"
Varicose Veins	Veins very close together

Ten Thousand Dollars

First doctor: "Why did you perform that operation on Mr. MacArthur?"

Second doctor: "Ten thousand dollars."

First doctor: "No. Perhaps you didn't hear me correctly. What did Mr. MacArthur have?"

Second doctor: "Ten thousand dollars."

Testimony

A testimony is what's left after the test.

Thanksgiving

I always call the turkey Napoleon, since I always get the bony part.

At Thanksgiving, what does a turkey have to be thankful for?

Theologian

There was a young theologian named Fiddle. He refused to accept his doctoral degree. He said, "It's bad enough being Fiddle, without being Fiddle, D.D."

The Other One

At an elegant dinner party, the hostess went all-out to present a fabulous meal. However, just before the dinner started, a little water was spilled onto the marble floor. When the waiter entered the dining room carrying a large, beautiful steamship roast, he slipped and fell flat, and the roast went flying to the floor.

The quick-thinking hostess blurted out, "No problem, Jason. Just take the roast back to the kitchen and bring out the other one."

Therapy

Everyone in Los Angeles is in therapy. It's a good thing there aren't parking spaces for the emotionally handicapped. There would be no place to park.

Things Parents Learn from Their Children

1. There is no such a thing as child-proofing your house.

2. If you spray hair spray on dust bunnies and run over them with roller blades, they ignite.

3. One four-year-old's voice is louder than 200 adults in a crowded restaurant.

4. You should not throw baseballs in the air when the ceiling fan is on.

5. The glass in today's windows (even the double-pane ones) doesn't stop a baseball hit by a ceiling fan.

6. When the sound of a toilet flushing is followed by the words "Uh-oh," it's already too late.

7. Brake fluid mixed with Clorox makes smoke—lots of it.

8. When you use a waterbed as home plate and it's hit by someone wearing baseball shoes, the mattress does not merely leak. It explodes.

9. A king-size waterbed holds enough water to fill a 2000-square-foot house four inches deep.

10. "Play-Doh" and *microwave* should never be used in the same sentence.

11. No matter how much Jell-O mix you pour into a swimming pool, you still can't walk on water.

12. VCRs do not eject peanut butter and jelly sandwiches, even though TV commercials make it appear that they do.

13. Marbles dropped into a car's gas tank make lots of noise when you're driving.

14. Always look in the oven before you turn it on.

15. Plastic toys do not like ovens.

16. The spin cycle on the washing machine does not make earth worms dizzy.

17. It will, however, make cats dizzy.

18. Cats throw up twice their body weight when they get dizzy.

Thirty-five

A woman visited her doctor and asked if a woman should have children after thirty-five. I said, "Thirty-five children is enough for any woman!"

Gracie Allen

Tickle

"Oh, Wilbur...when we were first married, you used to tickle my chin. Do it again!"

"Which one?"

Ties

Q: Which country makes the best ties?

A: Thailand, of course.

Tightwad

Did you hear about the Scotsman who quit golf, then took it up again twelve years later? He found his ball.

Time

The best way to kill time is to work it to death.

A watch repairman is someone you see when you don't have the time.

Times

Did you hear about the man who would wipe his wet shoes on the *New York Times?* You might say that for him, the newspaper was the *Times* that dry men's soles.

Tongue

The human tongue is only a few inches from the brain, but when some people talk, they seem miles apart.

Tooth and Nail

Show me a couple with high dental and manicure bills, and I'll show you a couple who's always fighting tooth and nail.

Toupee

You could you say a person who wears a toupee lives under an assumed mane.

Train of Thought

When someone wants you to follow his train of thought, make sure he doesn't have a loco motive.

Tranquilizer

The tranquilizer is one of America's leading composers.

Trouble

In the old days, when a youngster was in the principal's office, it meant the youngster was in trouble. Now, it means the principal is in trouble.

Trowel

When bricklayers retire, they throw in the trowel.

Truth

If you tell the truth, you don't have to have a good memory.

"Do you swear to tell the truth, the whole truth, and nothing but the truth, so help you God?" asked a bailiff as he swore in a witness at a trial.

"If I could tell the truth, the whole truth, and nothing but the truth," the witness responded, "I would be God!"

Turkey

He who wants to soar with eagles must avoid running with the turkeys.

Two Fingers

A third-grade teacher told her class on the first day of school, "When you need to be excused to go to the bathroom, just hold up two fingers."

A little boy in the back row said, "I don't see how that's going to help a bit."

Two Spiders

Are two spiders who just got married called newly webs?

Umbrella

"Your umbrella looks as though it's seen better days."
"It has had its ups and downs."

Undertaker

Teacher: "Donald, who said, 'Give me liberty or give me death?'"

Student: "Patrick Henry."

Teacher: "That's right. Who said, 'I have come to bury Caesar, not to praise him?'"

Student: "The undertaker."

Unpopular

The best way to be unpopular is to set a good example.

Unspeakable

It took about 50 years for movies to go from silent to unspeakable.

Valor

Valor is to travel on an ocean liner without tipping. Discretion is to come back on a different ship.

Value of Money

The best way to make kids understand the value of money is to charge stuff to their credit cards.

Vegetables

If you eat your vegetables for 85 years, you won't die young.

Vein

The doctor kept giving me medications for my severe cold. However, they were all in vein.

Vet

Is it true that a retired army animal doctor is called a vet vet?

Wacky Questions

Can a man be arrested for striking a match?

Do people in water beds sleep in life jackets?

Do they have coffee breaks at tea companies?

Do you call a plumber's assistant a drainee?

Do you have to wear a tea-shirt while serving tea?

Do you know why days break and nights fall?

Does it hurt when you crack a joke?

Is it possible to sharpen your shoulder blades?

How do you travel to the four corners of the world if the world is round?

How come black cows eat green grass, make yellow butter, and give white milk?

How is it possible for a two-pound box of candy to make you gain five pounds?

How many loops are there in a loophole?

How much does a pound cake weigh?

How much does the Milky Way?

How much sand is in a sandwich?

How much scotch is in Scotch tape?

If a baker works in a bakery, where does a butcher work?

If a bride wears white for happiness, why does a groom wear black?

If a biscuit is a soda cracker, is an ice pick a water cracker?

If a cook gets his pay, what does a coffee urn?

If a draft passes through a bank, does it give the clerks a cold?

If a duck can swim, can a spar-row?

If a fiddle is wood, is a trom-bone?

If a fishnet catches fish, does a hairnet catch hair?

If a fortification is a large fort, is a ratification a large rat?

If a man doesn't like his aunt, is he an anti-aunty?

If a man eats dates, is he consuming time?

Waistline

A group of sedentary businessmen realized their waist-lines were getting larger, so they started up a lunch-hour workout session. They called their group "Middle Management."

Waiter, Waiter

Customer: "Waiter! There's a fly in my soup."

Waiter: "If you throw it a pea, it'll play water polo."

Customer: "Waiter! How dare you splash soup on my trousers!"

Waiter: "I'm sorry sir, but now you've got soup in your fly."

Customer: "Waiter! There's a fly in my soup."

Waiter: "If you leave it there, the goldfish will eat it."

Customer: "Waiter! There's a fly in my soup."

Waiter: "I know sir! It's fly soup."

Customer: "Waiter! There's a fly in my soup."

Waiter: "Oh, dear. It must have committed insecticide."

Washington, DC

If I ever go crazy, I hope it will happen in Washington. I won't be noticed there.

Watch

"Please run upstairs and get my watch."

"Maybe it will run down by itself."

"No, it won't. We have a winding staircase."

"I once swallowed a watch."

"Wasn't that considered time-consuming?"

Weather

On cable television there is a channel that gives you 24 hours of weather. We had something like that when I was growing up. We called it a window.

Wedding

Weddings have become so expensive that now it's the father who breaks down and cries.

A wedding usually means showers for the bride and curtains for the groom.

Weevils

Two boll weevils came to town to make their fortunes. One worked hard and eventually became rich and famous. The other was always lazy, so he remained the lesser of two weevils.

Weight Reduction

I have found a good weight reduction exercise. It consists of placing both hands against the edge of the table and pushing back.

Weight Watchers

Is it true that the owners of Weight Watchers are living off the fat of the land?

Whale of a Tail

Sunday school teacher: "What lesson do we learn from the story of Jonah and the whale?"

Student: "People make whales sick."

Whatever

Man: "Whatever I say goes."

Woman: "Please talk to yourself."

What's in a Name?

She calls it a purse, but I call it a portable attic.

It got so bad that I didn't have a dime to my name—so I changed my name.

You can call a woman a kitten but not a cat, a mouse but not a rat, a chicken but not a hen, a duck but not a goose, a vision but not a sight.

What Women Want

Original list (age 22):

1. Handsome
2. Charming
3. Financially successful
4. A caring listener
5. Witty
6. In good shape

7. Dresses with style

8. Appreciates finer things

9. Full of thoughtful surprises

10. An imaginative, romantic lover

Revised list (age 32):

1. Nice looking (prefer hair on his head)

2. Opens car doors, holds chairs

3. Has enough money for a nice dinner

4. Listens more than talks

5. Laughs at my jokes

6. Carries bags of groceries with ease

7. Owns at least one tie

8. Appreciates a good home-cooked meal

9. Remembers birthdays and anniversaries

10. Seeks romance at least once a week

Revised list (age 42):

1. Not too ugly (bald head okay)

2. Doesn't drive off until I'm in the car

3. Works steady; splurges on dinner out occasionally

4. Nods head when I'm talking

5. Usually remembers punch lines of jokes

6. Is in good enough shape to rearrange the furniture

7. Wears a shirt that covers his stomach

8. Knows not to buy champagne with screw-top caps

9. Remembers to put the toilet seat down

10. Shaves most weekends

Revised list (age 52):

1. Keeps hair in nose and ears trimmed
2. Doesn't belch or scratch in public
3. Doesn't borrow money too often
4. Doesn't nod off to sleep when I'm venting
5. Doesn't retell the same joke too many times
6. Is in good enough shape to get off couch on weekends
7. Usually wears matching socks and fresh underwear
8. Appreciates a good TV dinner
9. Remembers my name on occasion
10. Shaves some weekends

Revised list (age 62):

1. Doesn't scare small children
2. Remembers where bathroom is
3. Doesn't require much money for upkeep
4. Only snores lightly when asleep
5. Remembers why he's laughing
6. Is in good enough shape to stand up by himself
7. Usually wears clothes
8. Likes soft foods
9. Remembers where he left his teeth
10. Remembers that it's the weekend

Revised list (age 72):

1. Breathing
2. Doesn't miss the toilet

Why

Q: Why did the chicken cross the road?

A: That's an eggs-istential question.

Why God Made Moms

Answers that elementary-school-age children gave to the following questions:

Why did God make mothers?

1. She's the only one who knows where the Scotch tape is.

2. Mostly to clean the house.

3. To help us out of there when we were getting born.

How did God make mothers?

1. He used dirt, just like for the rest of us.

2. Magic plus superpowers and a lot of stirring.

3. God made my mom just the same like he made me. He just used bigger parts.

What ingredients are mothers made of?

1. God makes mothers out of clouds and angel hair and everything nice in the world and one dab of mean.

2. They had to get their start from men's bones. Then they mostly use string, I think.

Why did God give you your mother and not some other mom?

1. We're related.

2. God knew she likes me a lot more than other people's moms like me.

What kind of little girl was your mom?

1. My mom has always been my mom and none of that other stuff.

2. I don't know because I wasn't there, but my guess would be pretty bossy.

3. They say she used to be nice.

What did mom need to know about dad before she married him?

1. His last name.

2. She had to know his background. Like, is he a crook? Does he get drunk on beer?

3. Does he make at least eight hundred dollars a year? Does he say no to drugs and yes to chores?

Why did your mom marry your dad?

1. My dad makes the best spaghetti in the world. And my mom eats a lot.

2. She got too old to do anything else with him.

3. My grandma says that mom didn't have her thinking cap on.

Who's the boss at your house?

1. Mom doesn't want to be the boss, but she has to because dad's such a goofball.

2. Mom. You can tell by her room inspection. She sees the stuff under the bed.

3. I guess Mom is, but only because she has a lot more to do than Dad.

What's the difference between moms and dads?

1. Moms work at work and work at home, and dads just go to work at work.

2. Moms know how to talk to teachers without scaring them.

3. Dads are taller and stronger, but moms have all the real power because that's who you got to ask if you want to sleep over at your friend's.

4. Moms have magic; they make you feel better without medicine.

What does your mom do in her spare time?

1. Mothers don't do spare time.

2. To hear her tell it, she pays bills all day long.

What would it take to make your mom perfect?

1. On the inside she's already perfect. Outside, I think some kind of plastic surgery.

2. Diet. You know, her hair. I'd diet, maybe blue.

*If you could change one thing about your mom,
what would it be?*

1. She has this weird thing about me keeping my room clean. I'd get rid of that.

2. I'd make my mom smarter. Then she would know it was my sister who did it and not me.

3. I would like for her to get rid of those invisible eyes in the back of her head.

Wilt

Preacher: "Wilt thou take this woman as thy lawful wedded wife?"

Groom: "I wilt."

Wisdom

I have learned silence from the talkative, tolerance from the intolerant, and kindness from the unkind.

Wisdom Teeth

Wisdom teeth are what develop when you bite off more than you can chew.

They call them wisdom teeth because taking them out helps pay for the dentist's kids' education.

Without a Collar

A priest went to a little backwoods town during his vacation. A local fellow engaged him in conversation, and when he found he was a priest, he said, "My lay church group is having a meeting tonight, and we'd love to have you speak to us."

The priest said he would speak, but then remembered

that he had not brought a clerical collar with him. So he went to the local priest, explained his situation, and asked if he might borrow a collar.

The other priest nodded and said, "I understand your situation: a lay date and a collar short."

Wolf

The playful, middle-aged wolf sidled up to the brunette. "Where have you been all my life?" he asked.

She looked at him coolly and replied, "Well, for the first half of it, I wasn't born."

Woman Driver

If you don't like the way a woman drives, get off the sidewalk.

Women

On one issue, at least, men and women agree: They both distrust women.

Wooden Leg

My uncle has a wooden leg.
My aunt has a cedar chest.

Work

It takes some people an hour to get to work—after they get there.

Judge: "What good have you ever done for society?"

Robber: "Well, I've kept four or five detectives working regularly."

When it comes to work, there are many who will stop at nothing.

According to the latest statistics, there are 60 million Americans who aren't working. And there are plenty more if you count the ones with jobs.

Wounds

If time really did heal all wounds, doctors wouldn't keep you in the waiting room so long.

Writing

There is a book for people who disagree—it's called a *contradictionary*.

Wrong

You have your shoes on the wrong feet.

But these are the only feet I have.

It's easy enough to be pleasant
   When everything goes like a song;
But the man worthwhile
   Is the man who can smile
When everything seems to go wrong.

Young

You're young only once, but if you keep the same wardrobe, you can look foolish forever.

Youth

You're a youth only once. After that, it takes another excuse.

Zoo

I had to buy two tickets at the zoo—one to get in, and one to get out.

Other Books by Bob Phillips